GREAT

KITCHEN
IDEAS

MEREDITH BOOKS

DES MOINES, IOWA

Great Kitchen Ideas
Editor: Vicki Christian
Contributing Project Manager/Writer: Jody Garlock
Associate Design Director: Som Inthalangsy
Contributing Graphic Designer: David Jordan, Studio 22
Copy Chief: Terri Fredrickson
Copy Editor: Kevin Cox
Publishing Operations Manager: Karen Schirm
Senior Editor, Asset and Information Management: Phillip Morgan
Edit and Design Production Coordinator: Mary Lee Gavin
Editorial Assistant: Kaye Chabot
Book Production Managers: Pam Kvitne, Marjorie J. Schenkelberg, Rick von Holdt, Mark Weaver
Imaging Center Operator: Vicki A. Morlan
Contributing Copy Editor: Nancy Ginzel
Contributing Proofreaders: Kristi Berg, Julie Collins, Judith Stern Friedman,
Contributing Cover Photographer: Gordon Beall
Contributing Indexer: Stephanie Reymann

Meredith® Books
Editor in Chief: Gregory H. Kayko
Executive Director, Design: Matt Strelecki
Managing Editor: Amy Tincher-Durik
Executive Editor: Benjamin W. Allen
Senior Editor/Group Manager: Vicki Leigh Ingham
Senior Associate Design Director: Ken Carlson
Marketing Product Manager: Brent Wiersma

Editorial Director: Linda Raglan Cunningham
Executive Director, Marketing: Kevin Kacere
Executive Director, New Business Development: Todd M. Davis
Executive Director, Sales: Ken Zagor
Director, Operations: George A. Susral
Director, Production: Douglas M. Johnston
Director, Marketing: Amy Nichols
Business Director: Jim Leonard

Vice President and General Manager: Douglas J. Guendel

Meredith Publishing Group
President: Jack Griffin
Senior Vice President: Karla Jeffries

Meredith Corporation
Chairman of the Board: William T. Kerr
President and Chief Executive Officer: Stephen M. Lacy

In Memoriam: E.T. Meredith III (1933–2003)

All of us at Meredith® Books are dedicated to providing you with information and ideas to enhance your home. We welcome your comments and suggestions. Write to us at: Meredith Books, Home Decorating and Design Editorial Department, 1716 Locust St., Des Moines, IA 50309-3023.

GREAT
KITCHEN
IDEAS

CHAPTER 1
Kitchen Trends

What's cooking in today's kitchens? This showcase, starting on page 8, offers inspiration and gives a glimpse of up-to-the-minute styles and concepts.

CHAPTER 2
Classic Elegance

CHAPTER 5

Country-Style Comfort

248

190

CHAPTER 6
Global Influence

240

Kitchen Trends

1

Designers are throwing curves INTO KITCHENS, BREAKING UP THE CONVENTIONAL STRAIGHT AND BOXY LOOK IN SOFT, NEW WAYS. ROUNDED SINKS, CURVED FAUCETS, BOWED CABINETRY, AND CURVACEOUS ISLANDS ARE CHANGING THE SHAPE—AND FEEL—OF USUALLY LINEAR SPACES. ON THIS ISLAND STAINLESS-STEEL CYLINDERS ROUND OUT TWO CORNERS FOR A PLEASANT DEPARTURE FROM THE EXPECTED.

A dash of this, A PINCH OF THAT. A UNIQUE AND SOMETIMES
SURPRISING MIX OF STYLES FLAVORS 21ST-CENTURY KITCHENS. ALMOST ANYTHING
GOES. IN THIS REMODELED KITCHEN, EXPOSED-BRICK WALLS MINGLE CONTENTEDLY
WITH MODERN STAINLESS STEEL AND AN ARCH-SHAPE SMOKY GLASS BACKSPLASH
THAT'S A LITTLE '70S. SUCH JUXTAPOSITIONS IN MATERIALS, STYLES, AND ERAS GIVE
THE FAVORITE ROOM OF THE HOME ITS OWN BRAND OF CHARACTER AND INTRIGUE.

Exquisite flourishes ON CABINETS AND ISLANDS CREATE THE LOOK OF FINE FURNITURE. IN THIS KITCHEN TAKE AWAY THE DECORATIVE BRACKETS BELOW THE CABINETS AND THE LOOK IS MERELY STATUS QUO. WITH THE BRACKETS IN PLACE, THE CABINETS APPEAR GRANDER. LOWER CABINETRY ALSO GETS IN ON THE ACTION, WITH FURNITURE-STYLE FEET ADDED TO THE TOE-KICKS. AS IS USUALLY THE CASE, ATTENTION TO DETAIL IS WHAT TRANSFORMS AN ORDINARY SPACE INTO A SHOWPLACE.

Artful imagery AND EVER-GROWING MATERIALS CHOICES HAVE MADE
THE ONCE-HUMBLE FARMHOUSE SINK A FASHIONABLE OPTION. ALSO CALLED APRON-
FRONT SINKS, THE DEEP, WIDE BASINS POPULARIZED IN 1900S RURAL AMERICA HAVE
SHED THEIR PLAIN WHITE PORCELAIN FORMS FOR STAINLESS STEEL, SLATE, GRANITE,
COPPER, AND OTHER SLEEK AND TEXTURAL MATERIALS. EVEN WHEN RETAINING
A COUNTRY LOOK IN CLASSIC WHITE, FINE DETAILING—SUCH AS THIS PHEASANT
IMAGERY AND MOLDED DESIGNS—BRINGS A DELIGHTFUL LOOK TO AN OLD FAVORITE.

Restaurant-inspired amenities GIVE GOURMETS—AS WELL AS COOKS WHO MERELY DABBLE—AN EXTRA LEVEL OF CONVENIENCE. POT-FILLER FAUCETS, FOR EXAMPLE, FILL THE BILL FOR CONVENIENCE AS WELL AS STYLE. INSTEAD OF TOTING HEAVY WATER-FILLED POTS FROM THE SINK, COOKS CAN SIMPLY FILL 'ER UP AT THE COOKTOP. INTEGRATED INTO THE WALL, THIS FAUCET SHIMMERS AGAINST A BACKDROP OF GLASS TILE. OTHER POPULAR GOURMET TOUCHES THAT TAKE THEIR CUE FROM RESTAURANTS INCLUDE TALL GOOSENECK-STYLE FAUCETS AND GLASS-FRONT REFRIGERATORS. BEFORE LONG, EATING IN MAY BE THE REAL TREAT.

Well-placed indulgences CAN TRANSFORM A ROOM. SUCH IS THE CASE WITH ISLAND COUNTERTOPS, WHICH STEP OUT IN SHOWY SURFACES AND PUNCHY COLORS THAT PROVIDE A WOW FACTOR. THE TREND TOWARD EXOTIC AND COLORFUL PLAYS OUT ON THIS ISLAND, WHERE GLACIAL BLUE GLAZED LAVA STONE SHINES AGAINST PALE BLUE GLASS TILES ON THE COLUMN. MORE CONVENTIONAL SURFACES SUCH AS QUARTZ CAN ALSO PROVIDE THE ALL-IMPORTANT ELEMENT OF SURPRISE WHEN THE COLOR IS BOLD AND UNEXPECTED.

Small but mighty BEST DESCRIBES A NEW WAVE OF DRAWER-STYLE APPLIANCES. DISHWASHER DRAWERS—USUALLY INSTALLED IN PAIRS—OFFER FLEXIBILITY TO RUN SMALL LOADS. WHEN THE DRAWERS FLANK THE SINK, AS IN THIS KITCHEN, THE HIGHER PLACEMENT MAKES FOR EASY LOADING AND UNLOADING. ALSO ON THE PULLOUT APPLIANCE FRONT, WARMING DRAWERS ARE MAKING COLD MEALS A THING OF THE PAST, AND REFRIGERATOR DRAWERS WITH KID-FRIENDLY ACCESSIBILITY ARE FREEING UP BEVERAGE AND SNACK SPACE IN THE MAIN FRIDGE.

It's out of sight AND OUT OF MIND FOR LAUNDRY AREAS. WASHERS AND DRYERS ARE FINDING NEW HOMES CONCEALED IN KITCHEN CABINETRY. ALTHOUGH BEST-SUITED FOR A PANTRY (TO REDUCE NOISE AND OFFER A DISCREET PLACE FOR DIRTY LAUNDRY), IN SOME KITCHENS WASHERS AND DRYERS FIT RIGHT INTO THE CORE WORK ZONE. A REMOVABLE TOE-KICK ALLOWS THESE BUILT-IN FRONT-LOADING UNITS TO BE PULLED OUT FOR SERVICING. HOW'S THAT FOR CONVENIENCE?

An open-minded approach PUTS A LIGHT SPIN ON KITCHENS, THANKS TO SHELVES THAT SUPPLEMENT OR EVEN REPLACE UPPER CABINETS. THESE BRACKETED SHELVES HUNG AGAINST BEADED BOARD STRIKE A NOSTALGIC NOTE, BUT THE LOOK EASILY SHIFTS TO CONTEMPORARY WITH STAINLESS-STEEL "FLOATING" SHELVES AGAINST A PLAIN WALL. ALONG WITH EVERYDAY DISHES, TREASURED COLLECTIONS ARE BEING PUT ON DISPLAY—BRINGING A DESERVING DECORATIVE TOUCH TO A ROOM THAT UNTIL RECENT YEARS WAS ALL ABOUT FUNCTION.

What's new is old WITH STOVES AND REFRIGERATORS. REMODELING PURISTS WHO WANT TO GIVE THEIR OLD HOMES A COMFORTING CONNECTION TO THE PAST CLAMOR OVER RANGES THAT MIMIC COOKSTOVES AND PANELED FRIDGES THAT RESEMBLE ICEBOXES. EVEN REAL-DEAL APPLIANCES FROM THE '40S AND '50S ARE BEING CALLED BACK INTO ACTION IN SOME KITCHENS. THERE'S ONE BIG DIFFERENCE WITH REPRODUCTIONS SUCH AS THIS RANGE, THOUGH: THEY'RE FULLY LOADED WITH MODERN CONVENIENCES.

A place for everything AND EVERYTHING IN ITS PLACE IS THE MANTRA FOR ULTRA-ORGANIZED KITCHENS. BEHIND DOORS AND DRAWERS, CUSTOM-SIZE SHELVES, SLOTS, AND TRAYS CRADLE CUTTING BOARDS, COOKIE SHEETS, KNIVES, AND MORE. THESE LITTLE ORGANIZATIONAL EXTRAS ADD A GREAT DEAL OF FUNCTION AND ARE OFTEN WHAT HOMEOWNERS END UP LOVING THE MOST. A GREAT-LOOKING KITCHEN IS NOTHING IF FAVORITE GADGETS ARE LOST IN THE SHUFFLE.

Lighting is eye candy FOR THE KITCHEN—A SUMPTUOUS FINISHING TOUCH. HUNG AS A TRIO THESE SHAPELY GLASS PENDANTS PROVIDE A BIG SCULPTURAL BOOST IN ADDITION TO BEING AN IDEAL SOURCE OF TASK LIGHTING. THE REAL BEAUTY OF PENDANTS—WHETHER THEY'RE MINIATURES HUNG ABOVE AN ISLAND OR BOWL-STYLE FIXTURES ABOVE A TABLE—IS THAT THEY OFFER A CHANCE TO BE CREATIVE AND BRING IN SOME DRAMA WITH MINIMAL EFFORT AND COST.

Classic Elegance

2

Comfort Zoned

SUBDIVIDING A LARGE KITCHEN INTO WELL-DEFINED AREAS CREATES AN APPROACHABLE AND INVITING ROOM FOR ADDRESSING THE TASKS AT HAND.

LEFT: A TROWELED AND WAXED MIX OF PLASTER AND MARBLE DUST GIVES WALLS AN OLD-WORLD LOOK.

OPPOSITE: FRAMED BY DRAPERIES, THE DINING AREA GAINS A SENSE OF PROMINENCE. VELVET LOUNGE CHAIRS, AN EMPIRE ROSEWOOD TABLE, AND A COMFY SOFA SET THE MOOD FOR FINE DINING.

Comfort Zoned

TUMBLED TRAVERTINE FLOORING UNIFIES THIS THREE-ROOM KITCHEN. MARBLEIZED LIMESTONE ON THE ISLAND SHARES A SLEEKNESS WITH THE APPLIANCES. THE STIR-FRYING STATION'S BACKSPLASH DESIGN IS REPEATED IN THE PRIMARY COOKING AREA.

A large kitchen tops many homeowners' wish lists, and at 900 square feet this kitchen may have seemed like a dream come true. But the reality is that it takes foresight to turn a cavernous space into a warm and functional hub. The plan here? Divide and conquer. By carving the large room into smaller work zones, the square footage is easy to navigate.

Although the layout retains its openness, putting up a few walls establishes key boundaries between work and relaxation. The largest area remains a hardworking cooking space, while a smaller room with a wide doorway becomes a lounge for thumbing through cookbooks or planning parties. The existing sitting area just off the kitchen forms a third room, used as the dining area.

The still-large main space takes a similar focused approach, although it defines areas without walls. One area is designated as the primary cooking zone; another becomes a secondary station for stir-frying. There's also an office area, a cleanup station, and a baking hub. The huge island unifies the different zones—and is neutral territory where everyone comes together at the end of a busy day.

LEFT: STATELY PILASTERS DEFINE THE
COOKING AREA. THE RANGE BACKSPLASH
IS COVERED IN LIMESTONE, ECHOING THE
PERIMETER COUNTERTOP SURFACES. INLAID
STARS OF LIMESTONE AND BLACK MARBLE
CREATE THE BACKSPLASH'S QUILTED DESIGN.

ABOVE: THE VEGETABLE SINK BRINGS ADDED
FUNCTION TO THE ISLAND. THE HAMMERED-
COPPER BOWL AND FRENCH BRASS PLUMBING
FIXTURE WILL AGE BEAUTIFULLY.

ABOVE: THE OFFICE AREA INCLUDES A DESK AND CABINETS THAT HIDE AN AUDIO-VIDEO CENTER. HIGH CABINETS ARE ACCESSIBLE VIA THE LADDER.

OPPOSITE: GLASS-FRONT CABINETS BOUNCE LIGHT AROUND A SECTION OF THE KITCHEN THAT SERVES AS A COOK'S LOUNGE. THE ANTIQUE TABLE USED AS AN ISLAND PROVIDES ADDITIONAL PREP AND SERVING SPACE. ORIENTAL RUGS ADD A LIVING ROOM QUALITY.

Collected Character

Formal touches such as English china pieces and Italian fabrics transform a compact kitchen into a polished gem.

Left: Sheets of inch-square tiles create a period-inspired pattern on the floor.

Opposite: A collection of Blue Willow china launches the kitchen's classic color scheme. The range hood's mantel provides a pleasing view from other rooms.

COLLECTED CHARACTER

A small kitchen can still be grand. In this condominium style trumps size. Borrowing architectural and decorative concepts from other rooms, the size-challenged space shares the formal elegance that weaves through the home.

Traditional English china pieces power the room's classic blue-and-white color scheme. Although the collection of plates, vases, and bowls would more often reside in a formal dining room, they're front and center in this kitchen. So is the range hood mantel, which is modeled after the fireplace in the living room. And the turned legs on the island echo the style of an antique end table in another room.

Not all dishes merit display though. Pleated fabric panels conceal everyday items, as well as a few collectibles, stored in the glass-front cabinets. The blue-and-white Italian fabric functions like window drapery, visually softening the room and adding unexpected detailing.

To fit with the fine fabric and china, the kitchen's surfaces are high-quality as well. Perimeter countertops are statuary marble, the purest and whitest variety available. The black granite on the island is like an exclamation point—a declaration that a small kitchen can enjoy the finer things.

LEFT: FABRIC PANELS
ATTACHED TO THE
INSIDE OF GLASS-
FRONT DOORS
VISUALLY SOFTEN
THE CABINETS. THE
PATTERN'S REPEAT
IS CENTERED ON THE
FRONT OF EACH PANE
FOR A POLISHED LOOK.

OPPOSITE: LIGHT
FROM A WINDOW
ENERGIZES THE
REFLECTIVE
SURFACES, INCLUDING
THE GLOSSY TILE
BACKSPLASH AND
THE SATIN FINISH
ON THE PAINTED
CABINETS. ABOVE THE
RANGE EMBOSSED
CELTIC-PATTERN TILE
BECOMES A SUBTLE
ART PIECE.

French Blend

Merging a love of tradition with a fondness for European-inspired character, this elegant kitchen is a culinary delight.

Left: The apron-front sink has capacity and character. It is carved from Mexican travertine, which blends beautifully with the Italian marble used for countertops.

Opposite: Crown molding helps the cabinets stand out against the stucco and cast-stone range hood. A pot-filler faucet on the range backsplash offers cooking convenience.

French Blend

THE LAYOUT OF THIS 1920S KITCHEN CENTERS AROUND THE ISLAND—A MODERN ELEMENT WITH A DISTRESSED FINISH THAT HONORS THE PAST. THE ISLAND'S CURVACEOUS COUNTERTOP AND CARVED SIDE PANELS VISUALLY SOFTEN THE ROOM'S STRONG ANGLES.

Like a confident cook who blends different recipes to come up with a signature dish, the most interesting kitchens tend to be a little bit of this and a little bit of that. Consider this kitchen a classic recipe with a French twist.

The main ingredient is the cabinetry, which features paneled doors and drawers and is topped with crown molding. Rich in character, the cabinets serve as a classic base. Earthy colors and stone surfaces season the room with French flair. The cabinetry is painted in celadon, the marble countertops are a peachy coral color, and the stone-tile backsplash wears a mottled mix of golds and beiges.

The kitchen is more than a beautiful stylistic blending though. With elegant facades playing a camouflage role, the room's utilitarian aspects are gracefully integrated. Cabinetry that resembles an armoire hides two refrigerators. Wood panels conceal a warming drawer and icemaker. A cast-stone arch disguises the ventilation system for the range, and substantial moldings and stepped soffits hide ductwork. With two sinks and a large center island designed for serious prep work, this kitchen is bound to inspire culinary creativity in the chef who is lucky enough to claim the space.

LEFT: ORIGINAL WINDOWS MAINTAIN THE HOME'S INTEGRITY. THE GAUZY WINDOW TREATMENTS VISUALLY SOFTEN THE ROOM'S HARD ELEMENTS WHILE ALLOWING LIGHT TO ENTER.

BELOW: THE BLACK FINISH AND CURVED ENDS OF THE SHELVING UNIT PLAY OFF THE ISLAND, WHILE THE CROWN MOLDING LINKS TO THE CABINETS AND GIVES THE SHELF ARCHITECTURAL PRESENCE.

ABOVE: A CRACKLE FINISH AND DARK GLAZE BRING RICHNESS AND DEPTH TO THE CABINETS. MOLDINGS ADD AN EXTRA LAYER OF FINE DETAILING.

OPPOSITE: SMALL APPLIANCES CONVENIENTLY RESIDE IN THE CORNER NEXT TO THE WIDE REFRIGERATOR, WHICH IS CONCEALED BY THE ARMOIRE-STYLE CABINETRY. CABINETS BELOW THE MICROWAVE DISGUISE AN ICEMAKER AND WINE COOLER.

Sky-High Lightness

A TWO-STORY DESIGN ELEVATES THIS KITCHEN TO NEW HEIGHTS. NATURAL COLORS AND TEXTURAL MATERIALS KEEP THE FOCUS ON THE ARCHITECTURE.

LEFT: A SMALL FREESTANDING CHEST ECHOES THE DETAILING ON THE GLASS-FRONT DOORS OF THE BUILT-IN CABINETS.

OPPOSITE: HEAVILY TEXTURED WALLS HEIGHTEN THE DRAMA OF THE TWO-STORY ROOM. THE NEUTRAL WALLS ACCENTUATE THE ARCHITECTURE, AND MARBLE FLOORING IS AN EARTHY COMPLEMENT.

Sky-High Lightness

Repetition gives the kitchen continuity. Glass-door cabinets echo the divided windows. The apron-front sink appears in a smaller version on the island. The stainless-steel light fixtures offer a modern contrast.

Tangible things such as showy surfaces and gourmet appliances don't always give a kitchen its all-important design drama. In this kitchen it's air. This is a space where sheer volume is nothing short of spectacular.

The ceiling rises an impressive two stories, and abundant windows and glass doors flood the room with natural light. The result is an enviably spacious and serene place for cooking, dining, and even relaxing. With a timeless and understated cream-and-white color scheme, serenity prevails and the focus remains on the architecture.

This savvy layout incorporates repeating diagonals designed to minimize the room's rectangular shape. Double ovens placed on a diagonal visually soften the lines in one corner, and a diagonal area sliced from the prep island forms a small sitting spot. A balcony overlooking the kitchen provides another layer of architectural interest; used as a library, the space also expands the kitchen's function.

Key work areas such as the cleanup and cooking zones are strategically placed to direct the eye to the room's most valuable commodity: the windows with their woodsy views. After all, if you have it, why not flaunt it?

SKY-HIGH LIGHTNESS

NATURAL ELEMENTS ABOUND IN THE
SITTING AREA, WHICH FEATURES A
STONE FIREPLACE. TUMBLED-MARBLE
FLOORING PICKS UP THE EARTHY HUES
OF THE STONE. THE PENINSULA THAT
HOUSES THE COOKTOP IS PLACED ON
THE DIAGONAL TO CAPTURE VIEWS OF
THE OUTDOORS AND THE DINING AREA.
TRANSOMS LINE THE CEILING, HELPING
TO BALANCE THE TWO-STORY HEIGHT.

SKY-HIGH LIGHTNESS

BELOW: BEADED BOARD LINKS UPPER AND LOWER CABINETS IN THE DESK AREA, WHICH IS DESIGNED TO RESEMBLE A HUTCH. SOLID DOORS KEEP COMPUTER EQUIPMENT OUT OF VIEW.

OPPOSITE: FOR A FURNITURE LOOK THE UPPER CABINETS FEATURE STACKED TRIM MOLDING ON THE TOP AND A TOE VALANCE AT THE BOTTOM. A DOUBLE-OGEE EDGE ADDS ELEGANT DETAIL TO THE COUNTERTOPS AND IS A HORIZONTAL COMPLEMENT TO THE BEADED BOARD ON THE ISLAND.

OPPOSITE: THE CORNER NICHE IS A WORKHORSE, INCORPORATING A WINE CHILLER, COFFEE BAR, AND PLATE STORAGE. GLASS DOORS THAT ENCLOSE THE TELEVISION SLIDE INTO THE OPENING FOR UNOBSTRUCTED VIEWING.

RIGHT: THE LAYOUT PLACES OVENS ON A DIAGONAL TO MAKE EFFICIENT USE OF AN AWKWARD CORNER. THE BONUS UPPER LEVEL HOUSES A LIBRARY FOR PORING OVER COOKBOOKS.

Happy Together

Melding the luxuries of fine dining with the rigors of cooking, this combination kitchen and dining room proves that you can have it both ways.

Left: What appears to be part of an antique table attached to the peninsula is actually a faux drawer set on rococo-style legs.

Opposite: A waxed Venetian plaster finish on the walls and ceiling reflects light. Inset tiles on the marble backsplash pick up the yellow of the walls and cabinets and the blue of the range.

Happy Together

THE DISTRESSED YELLOW FINISH ON THE CABINETS AND ISLAND, WHICH EMULATES AN ANTIQUE FRENCH COMMODE, BRIGHTENS THE DARK CHERRY. SILK CURTAINS AND AN ANTIQUE CHANDELIER ARE SURPRISING AND LUXURIOUS TOUCHES.

In the not-so-distant past, a formal dining room was almost a prerequisite. Few cooks would entertain the idea of hosting dinner parties or holiday meals in the kitchen. Now the present-day love affair with kitchens blurs the boundaries. As this space shows, it's simple to make the two rooms one.

With no wall separating the kitchen and dining room, the primary challenge was to refine the elements on the must-have list, such as cabinets, lighting, and appliances. Cabinets are treated like fine furniture. Most notably and cleverly rococo-style legs and a faux drawer front dress up the end of the peninsula. Lighting combines the ordinary—such as recessed can ceiling lights—with the unexpected—an antique crystal chandelier that drips elegance. Just one glimpse of the blue enamel range is enough to make guests realize that this kitchen prides itself on going beyond the status quo.

Despite being an all-in-one space, the kitchen isn't too matched—a strategic character-building move. The cabinetry, island, and freestanding furniture are done in different styles and finishes to give the room a convincing collected-over-time look. The overall aesthetic is similar to a dining room—or perhaps it's a kitchen that avoids being, well, too kitcheny.

LEFT: CABINETRY IN THE DINING AREA FUNCTIONS AS A BUTLER'S PANTRY. THE FULL-SERVICE BEVERAGE AREA INCLUDES WINE REFRIGERATORS AND A SINK. THE SHELVING UNIT AND A ROUND MIRROR ADD DECORATIVE TOUCHES.

BELOW: FOR CONTINUITY THE COUNTERTOPS AND APRON-FRONT SINK FEATURE THE SAME MARBLE, WHICH IS WHITER THAN THE USUAL GRAY-VEINED VARIETY. A BAND OF MARBLE TRIM AROUND THE BACK AND SIDES OF THE SINK PROVIDES A SEAMLESS TRANSITION.

Clearing the Way

Smart storage solutions, a streamlined design, and subdued colors give a hectic hub a welcoming sense of calm.

Left: There's little trouble determining what goes where in this ultra-organized kitchen. Its clever storage includes a niche in the island to keep paper towels handy but out of view.

Opposite: The kitchen's calm quality is a nod to Scandinavian design, which favors simplicity. Backsplash tiles portray formal garden elements.

THE SAVVY LAYOUT
DIRECTS STORAGE TO
INTERIOR WALLS AND
THE ISLAND, FREEING
THE BACK WALL FOR
WINDOWS. PLACING
THE SINK IN THE ISLAND
CONSERVES LIMITED
COUNTER SPACE.

Repository is a fitting description for today's kitchens.
They're miniwarehouses for a growing number of gadgets
such as gourmet coffeemakers and televisions—in addition
to the usual pots and pans.

On the surface the quiet colors are what usher this room
into a state of tranquility. The primarily white-on-white
scheme is easy on the eye and provides visual continuity.
From a style standpoint the room pits traditional against
country—with a Scandinavian twist—but avoids being
jarring. The cabinetry, for example, features classic paneled
fronts with clean, Shaker simplicity.

While subtlety is key in this streamlined space, what
goes on behind closed doors and drawers really promotes
order. Compartments in cabinets and drawers are sized to
fit their contents, whether they store spices or flatware.
The smart storage extends to small appliances, which find
a custom fit in a cabinet at the end of the island. Even the
television, which is on the verge of becoming a kitchen
staple, is discreetly tucked into the island. It all adds up to a
contemplative space where order and light cut through the
clutter of daily life.

LEFT: CABINETS REACH THE CEILING TO PROVIDE PLENTIFUL STORAGE. THE ARCH-TOP CABINETRY HOUSING THE OVENS AND REFRIGERATORS, WHICH ARE HIDDEN BY PANELS, BREAKS UP THE BOXINESS. FOR BALANCE THE ARCHED CABINETRY REPEATS ON THE OPPOSITE WALL.

BELOW: A DRAWER IN THE ISLAND IS OUTFITTED WITH DOWELS WHERE TABLE LINENS CAN HANG TO MINIMIZE WRINKLES. IT ALSO HAS SPACE TO STACK TOWELS.

BELOW: ISLAND CUBBIES ARE STRATEGICALLY SIZED FOR COOKBOOKS AND A FLAT-PANEL TELEVISION, WHICH IS VISIBLE FROM THE BANQUETTE. THE DRAWER STORES LINENS.

OPPOSITE: THERE'S STORAGE GALORE IN THIS WALL OF CABINETS DESIGNED TO RESEMBLE A CHINA HUTCH. BEAMS ON THE CEILING ECHO THE GRID DESIGN OF THE GLASS-FRONT CABINET DOORS.

OPPOSITE: A BUMPOUT ON THE EXTERIOR WALL ALLOWS SPACE FOR A BANQUETTE. THE WINDOW SEAT BASE PROVIDES STORAGE, WHILE AN ANTIQUE TABLE BRINGS RUSTIC FLAIR TO THE CLASSIC SPACE.

BELOW: TO FREE COUNTERTOP SPACE THE COFFEEMAKER IS BUILT INTO THE CABINETRY. SLIM PULLOUT CABINETS THAT FLANK THE COFFEEMAKER STORE TEAS AND SUPPLIES FOR BEVERAGES.

OPPOSITE: CHINA AND
SILVER PIECES STAND
OUT AGAINST THE BLUE-
PAINTED CABINET INTERIOR.
RECESSED LIGHTS
ILLUMINATE THE DISPLAY.

TOP LEFT: SHELVES ARE
SIZED TO FIT DRINKING
GLASSES, PITCHERS, AND
OTHER CHINA PIECES. LESS-
USED ITEMS GO ON THE
HIGHER SHELVES.

BOTTOM LEFT: CUSTOM
COMPARTMENTS KEEP THIS
SILVERWARE COLLECTION
ORDERLY AND ACCESSIBLE.

Worthy Indulgence

Layered with crystal chandeliers and intricate millwork, this room proves that a hardworking kitchen doesn't have to skip the exquisite.

Left: Cut-glass crystals and pear-shape amber baubles detail the formal Italian chandeliers.

Opposite: A custom-carved cornice elegantly frames the large bay window. Lower cabinetry panels flanking the sink conceal the dishwashers.

WORTHY INDULGENCE

FINELY CRAFTED
CABINETRY WITH AN
ANTIQUE FINISH AND
AN APRON-FRONT SINK
DISPLAY EUROPEAN
INFLUENCE. MATCHING
CHANDELIERS AND
ORNATELY FRAMED
PAINTINGS ADD A LAYER
OF OPULENCE.

Why not make the kitchen worthy of a chandelier? It's a concept this luxurious space takes to heart. Italian crystal chandeliers exude elegance and send a signal that this kitchen dares to indulge in the finer things.

The room owes its distinguished ambience to classic details. Fluted columns, carved corbels, and elaborate moldings accent the cabinetry for architectural presence. The buttery yellow cabinetry, custom-made in Europe, was antiqued on site. It's a relatively easy decorative touch that helps the cabinets look more like fine antiques than basic storage units. Similarly, the Jerusalem limestone countertops, backsplashes, and flooring are specially treated to achieve hard-as-granite durability and textural richness. The reflective surfaces, along with the soft hues, cast a rich glow, accentuating the details and allowing the room's more utilitarian aspects to take a backseat.

Like the twin chandeliers above the island, the room intrigues with its many focal points. Above the cooktop gilt-frame paintings delight. In upper cabinets the beveled glass does the same. Even the kitchen sink, with its graceful fluted apron front, is a step above the ordinary—yet another example that this kitchen grasps the notion that good design is in the details.

WORTHY INDULGENCE

BELOW: THE COOKTOP'S ORNATE HEARTH DESIGN RESEMBLES THOSE FOUND IN OLD ENGLISH MANORS. FRAMED PAINTINGS PROPPED ON THE MANTEL CONTRIBUTE A SENSE OF FORMALITY.

OPPOSITE: SOFT COLORS, SUCH AS THE PALE YELLOW ON THE FREESTANDING HUTCH, BRIGHTEN THE KITCHEN.

Vintage Appeal 3

Beautiful Blend

THE BEST OF THEN AND NOW COMBINE IN A COASTAL KITCHEN THAT HITS ITS STRIDE AS A MODERN SPACE WITH AN OLD SOUL.

LEFT: VINTAGE-INSPIRED BRASS DIALS CONTROL SEVEN BURNERS AND TWO OVENS ON THE SHOWPIECE FRENCH RANGE.

OPPOSITE: THE CUSTOM RANGE HOOD WITH RIVETED STRAPS BRINGS A CONTEMPORARY EDGE TO THE NOSTALGIC KITCHEN.

BEAUTIFUL BLEND

DURABLE STAINLESS-STEEL COUNTERTOPS CONTRAST WITH THE MARBLE-TOPPED ISLAND. A VINTAGE WAREHOUSE LIGHT ABOVE THE ISLAND PICKS UP THE ROOM'S INDUSTRIAL UNDERTONE, AND SHELVES ALTERNATE WITH CABINETS FOR AN UNFITTED LOOK.

Designers often advise listening to what a house says. In this 100-year-old beach house, the message was clear: Step back in time. The kitchen sported a 1970s renovation that was dated by today's standards but awkwardly decades ahead of the home. Now renovated to near period perfection—and given barefoot ease befitting the home's waterside locale— it's the kitchen this old home was always meant to have.

A mix of antiques and reproductions captures the essence of the early 1900s. Upper cabinets are backed with beaded board and fronted with wavy-glass doors creatively fashioned from $5 windows purchased at a salvage yard. Open shelving and schoolhouse lights usher in more period charm. Even the sounds are convincingly old-fashioned: Removing the closing mechanism from the screen door, for example, creates a days-gone-by slam.

Even the modern amenities hint at the past. The generously sized four-door commercial refrigerator mimics an icebox, albeit in sleek stainless steel. Stainless and marble countertops withstand use by a busy family with kids, yet sidestep a fussy look. And wood floors that can be swept easily of sand bring a comforting simplicity to the newly aged beachside beauty.

OPPOSITE: OPEN SHELVES BACKED BY BEVELED-EDGE SUBWAY TILE, FURNITURE-STYLE CABINETRY, BRUSHED NICKEL DOOR LATCHES, AND SCHOOLHOUSE LIGHT FIXTURES HELP THE KITCHEN APPEAR ORIGINAL TO THE EARLY-1900S HOME.

BELOW: HALF-WALLS OPEN ONE END OF THE KITCHEN TO OTHER ROOMS. THE BUILT-IN DESK MAKES GOOD USE OF ONE OF THE HALF-WALLS. THE MINT GREEN HUE ENLIVENS THE MOSTLY WHITE SETTING.

ABOVE: NEW PANELED COLUMNS ECHO THE HOME'S BEEFY ARCHITECTURE. THE HALF-WALLS OPEN THE KITCHEN TO ADJACENT LIVING AREAS WHILE MAINTAINING A SENSE OF ENCLOSURE COMMON IN OLD HOMES.

OPPOSITE: AN OLD-FASHIONED SLATE CHALKBOARD SERVES AS A MESSAGE CENTER ABOVE THE FIREPLACE. THE PAINTED FIREPLACE SURROUND MATCHES THE FLOOR, EBONIZED TO CAMOUFLAGE A PATCHWORK OF OAK AND FIR.

History Lesson

RETHINKING THE BOUNDARIES BETWEEN ORNATE AND MINIMAL, A CENTURY-OLD KITCHEN FINDS ITS BLISS SOMEWHERE IN THE MIDDLE.

LEFT: RUBBED-NICKEL CABINET PULLS HAVE A VINTAGE LOOK, EVEN THOUGH THEY'RE REPRODUCTIONS.

OPPOSITE: SET AGAINST MOSAIC TILES, THE RANGE HOOD COMMANDS ATTENTION. EXPOSED SHELVES BELOW THE COOKTOP KEEP LOWER CABINETRY FROM BECOMING A SEA OF SOLID WOOD.

FLOUR SUGA

BISCUITS

History Lesson

Shapely glass pendants are modern contrasts to the fancy trims on the island, shelves, and range hood. Porcelain tile replaces the unsalvageable original wood floor. The teak island top resists moisture.

Living in a historical home carries a certain responsibility—most notably in respecting the past. So how is it possible to square a desire for minimalism with a house that calls for ornamentation such as curlicues and gingerbread trim? Creative compromise is the solution in this kitchen, which bridges the gap between two very different styles and eras.

The lofty goal was to create a family space with subtle sophistication, simplicity, and sleekness—and do it in a way befitting a century-old home. Visually airing out the closed-in space was the first and most pronounced step toward era-respectful minimalism. An island with open storage takes the place of a traffic-blocking peninsula; its red finish is modern yet picks up the brick color on a nearby fireplace. On the walls shelves replace upper cabinetry. While the shelves answer the call for simplicity, their lacy scrollwork brackets nod to an era that favored ornamentation.

A quiet color scheme of white and grays forms a simple and soothing backdrop that is as appropriate for a century-old kitchen as it is for a modern one. A sweep of mosaic tile from the countertop to the ceiling gives the white room a gleam and forms a subtle geometric pattern that complements all the curlicues. In the end the contrasts put a fresh perspective on an old kitchen.

OPPOSITE: LIKE THE WALL SHELVES, THE ISLAND MIXES ORNATE TRIMS WITH OPEN STORAGE. CHROME BASKETS ARE BRIGHT CONTRASTS TO THE RUBBED-NICKEL PULLS.

LEFT: SCROLLWORK SHELF BRACKETS ARE PERIOD TOUCHES, YET THEIR OPEN DESIGN KEEPS THE OVERALL LOOK LIGHT.

BELOW: FOR THEIR EASE OF USE, SINGLE-LEVER FAUCETS WITH PULLOUT SPRAYS WIN OUT OVER OLD-STYLE FAUCETS. MARBLE COUNTERTOPS EVENTUALLY WILL SHOW THE NICKS OF A WELL-USED KITCHEN, MAKING THEM A GOOD CHOICE FOR AN OLD HOME.

Well-Crafted Comeback

Artisan touches and keen attention to detail restore the architectural integrity of this Arts and Crafts gem.

Left: Antique-looking hinges and nameplates give the paneled refrigerator the appearance of an old-fashioned icebox.

Opposite: Exquisite detailing comes forward in the cooking area. The handcrafted copper range hood is trimmed with blackened cast metal. The dark range reverses the scheme, using polished copper as the trim. Amber-veined granite countertops play off the copper touches.

Well-Crafted Comeback

FIR TIMBERS THAT ACCENTUATE THE ROOM'S PEAKED ROOFLINE ADD CEILING-LEVEL DRAMA. LEADED-GLASS WINDOWS TAKE PRECEDENCE OVER UPPER CABINETS; THE TWO UPPER CABINETS ARE PAINTED TO RECEDE INTO THE WALL.

Renovation purists certainly would approve of the new look of this 1923 kitchen. It's about as close to the real deal as a modern cooking space can get—right down to the icebox-inspired refrigerator.

The nostalgic design reflects the ideals of the Arts and Crafts era. It was a time when natural beauty, handcrafted details, and use of indigenous materials were the norm, not the exception. The high standards of the past play out here on several levels. The black walnut used for the cabinets is a native species. Local artisans designed the copper range hood. Exposed ceiling beams, leaded-glass windows, and rough plaster walls restore the architectural integrity that had been sacrificed over 80 years of updates.

Even the appliances, which easily cause the most preservation-minded renovation to look too modern, have a comforting connection to the past. Black walnut panels and old-fashioned hinges and latches transform the refrigerator/freezer into a vintage icebox—at least on the outside. Similarly the copper-trimmed range appears to be straight out of the 1920s; with gas and electric ovens, two warming drawers, and an indoor barbecue, it's totally 21st century. This kitchen proves that even reproductions are at home when attention to detail is the overriding theme.

LEFT: THE DINING AREA VEERS TOWARD MODERN WITH A CONTEMPORARY PAINTING AND UPHOLSTERED CHAIRS, BUT EARTHY HUES KEEP THINGS IN THE ARTS AND CRAFTS ERA. PILLOWS ADD COZINESS TO THE BUILT-IN BANQUETTE.

BELOW: PANELS CAN MAKE A REFRIGERATOR SEEM LIKE MERELY ANOTHER CABINET—IN SOME CASES. THE HARDWARE ON THESE PANELS GRANDLY ANNOUNCES THE PRESENCE OF THE ICEBOX—ALBEIT A MODERN VERSION.

Historical Meets Hip

Eyecatching yellow cabinetry gives a 1918 kitchen a new attitude, while a reconfigured floor plan opens up more possibilities.

Left: Dark green granite countertops give the vintage kitchen a sophisticated and modern edge. They also act as visual anchors against the white tile walls.

Opposite: The view from the newly opened and widened corridor captures the kitchen's vintage charm. A bevy of schoolhouse light fixtures are period-appropriate exclamation points.

THE COMPACT ISLAND
IS A WORKHORSE WITH
A TOP THAT EXTENDS
ON ONE SIDE TO ALLOW
SEATING. TO OPTIMIZE
THE ISLAND'S SIZE,
WALKWAYS BY THE RANGE
AND SINK ARE SEVERAL
INCHES NARROWER THAN
THE TYPICAL 42 INCHES.

Old school doesn't mean out of touch. With bold yellow cabinets, granite countertops, and touches of stainless steel, this kitchen has ultra-now edge—never mind that it's part of a 1918 bungalow. The trick to the give and take between past and present is simple: balance.

Take, for example, the room's standout feature, the cabinets. Although their assertive hue screams modern, their distressed finish takes them back in time. There's a similar effect with the stainless steel, thanks to silver radiators and schoolhouse light fixtures that are vintage counterpoints to the range hood and appliances. And the lack of upper cabinetry is made less contemporary by walls covered in subway tile, a vintage favorite.

Smart use of existing space reconciles the size disparity between modern hub-of-the-home kitchens and yesteryear's closed-in cooking spaces. Removing a wall between the walk-in pantry and a narrow back-entry hall creates a wide corridor—almost a miniature room—that increases the kitchen's square footage without having to build an addition. A wide refrigerator and a baking center find a home in the corridor, and floor-to-ceiling cabinetry reinterprets the function of the traditional walk-in pantry. The built-in pantry, like the kitchen itself, shows that history can be rewritten.

OPPOSITE: REMOVING THE WALL BETWEEN A WALK-IN PANTRY AND THE BACK HALL CREATES THIS FUNCTIONAL GALLEY. TEXTURED GLASS MODERNIZES SOME OF THE CABINETS.

ABOVE: THE FARMHOUSE SINK AND OLD-STYLE LEVER HANDLES ARE VINTAGE CONTRASTS TO THE SLEEK GRANITE COUNTERTOPS.

Historical Meets Hip

BELOW: STAINLESS-STEEL SHELVING AND UTENSIL RODS MOUNTED ON THE SUBWAY TILES CREATE AN INTERPLAY OF MODERN AND VINTAGE.

OPPOSITE: SHORT NEW WINDOWS TRANSFORM A WALL THAT WAS FORMERLY WASTED SPACE. THE ORIGINAL WINDOWSILLS FELL BELOW COUNTER HEIGHT, WHICH LEFT NO ROOM FOR THE BASE CABINETS, SINK, OR DISHWASHER THAT NOW FIT HERE.

Storybook Beginning

THIS NEW KITCHEN WRITES ITS OWN CHAPTER
AS A SOPHISTICATED SPACE WITH A PLAYFUL
SIDE. THE RESULT? A COTTAGE CLASSIC.

LEFT: THIS STORAGE-
SAVVY DESIGN
INCORPORATES
DRAWERS BELOW
THE WINDOW SEAT.
THE RED-CHECKED
CUSHION ENLIVENS
THE WHITE BUILT-INS.

OPPOSITE: WINNING
OUT OVER A DESK
AREA, THE CUSHIONED
WINDOW SEAT IS AN
IDEAL PLACE FOR A
YOUNG FAMILY TO
GATHER. DRAWERS
BELOW AND TO THE
SIDES OF THE SEAT
PROVIDE THE STORAGE
OF A DESK.

STORYBOOK BEGINNING

OVERSCALE ELEMENTS, SUCH AS THE CABINET KNOBS, RELAX THE ROOM'S FORMALITY, AS DOES THE MIX OF CHERRY AND MARBLE COUNTERTOPS. THE PANELED TREATMENT ON THE BACKSPLASHES IS A DETAIL COMMON TO EARLY-1900S HOMES.

When building new, one gets the chance to start fresh. Fresh, for this seaside home, means stepping back in time to create a sophisticated English cottage look that's remarkably relaxed, thanks to a fun-loving red-and-white scheme. If it sounds like a room that is rife with contradictions, it is—and that's the beauty.

The simple contrasts are most pronounced in the jaunty color scheme. A long red island and vintage-look stove visually warm the white cabinetry. Red-and-white-checked fabric on the window seat cushion echoes the checkerboard range backsplash—a playful touch that brings a bit of diner inspiration into the mix. More contrasts—glossy and matte surfaces, open and closed cabinetry, round and square shapes—do their own small part to energize the room.

Although the design is easygoing, the kitchen seamlessly flows into the more formal dining room thanks to furniture-style cabinet detailing, such as brackets and scrolled feet. And informal accents, including the tempting candy-filled jars that line one countertop, are child-friendly but still fun for adults. They're simply one little reminder that a kitchen needn't be all work and no play.

OPPOSITE: GLASS DOORS, CHERRY COUNTERTOPS, AND FURNITURE-STYLE FEET GIVE THIS BUILT-IN CABINET A FREESTANDING LOOK. YELLOW BEADED-BOARD WALLS ARE A SUNNY CONTRAST TO THE WHITE CABINETRY AND TRIM.

BELOW: INSTEAD OF AN APPLIANCE GARAGE WITH A ROLL-UP TOP, A CABINET IDENTICAL TO OTHERS IN THE KITCHEN IS SIZED FOR SMALL APPLIANCES. THE HEAVY MIXER IS EASILY ACCESSIBLE ON THE BOTTOM SHELF.

Below: The prep-sink faucet shines with period styling but offers modern single-handle function and a pullout side sprayer.

Opposite: Brass pulls brighten the lower island cabinets. The cherry top gleams with six coats of oil-base sealer that protect it from moisture.

ABOVE: A CHECKERBOARD-TILE BACKSPLASH PERKS UP THE RANGE AREA. SHINY UTENSILS DOUBLE AS ART ON THE INFORMAL AND FUNCTIONAL RAIL-SYSTEM STORAGE UNIT.

OPPOSITE: THE KITCHEN'S PLAYFUL SIDE IS EVIDENT IN CANDY-FILLED GLASS JARS, A RED FRENCH RANGE, AND CHECKERBOARD TILE.

OPPOSITE: EXPANDING ON THE CONCEPT OF CONCEALING REFRIGERATORS BEHIND CABINETRY PANELS, THIS VENTED BIFOLD DOOR HIDES THE WALL OVEN AND MICROWAVE OVEN. WITH THE DOORS CLOSED, THE UNIT RESEMBLES AN ARMOIRE.

ABOVE: THE ROOM'S SMART STORAGE INCLUDES THIS BOOKSHELF INCORPORATED INTO ONE SIDE OF THE BUILT-IN REFRIGERATOR CABINET. THE CROWN MOLDING EXTENDS INTO THE FORMAL DINING ROOM FOR CONTINUITY.

Tailored for Today

Proud of its past but ready for some modern multitasking, this remodeled kitchen embraces the idea of personal space.

Left: Reproduction cup pulls and beaded inset drawers are small details that lend old-time authenticity.

Opposite: The main island, which houses dishwasher drawers and a prep sink, squares off with the range to form a semiprivate cooking corridor. The refrigerator is a few steps down, so it's part of the cooking area and also accessible to noncooks.

PORTSMOUTH

TAILORED FOR TODAY

COUNTERTOPS OF HONED SLATE—THE SAME MATERIAL USED FOR THE SINK—RUN THROUGHOUT THE KITCHEN FOR A STREAMLINED LOOK. REPRODUCTION PENDANTS HANG ABOVE THE SINK.

If there's one thing a well-conceived kitchen layout does brilliantly, it's that it prevents people from tripping over one another. This remodeled kitchen is able to accommodate multiple cooks or family members who simply want to hang out or work on the computer—without sacrificing the home's 1870s character.

Self-sufficiency tops the list of pluses in this efficient design. Instead of centering everything around a key feature, such as an island, the plan calls for decentralization. Areas for cooking, cleaning, and computing are spread out across the large room, giving each task personal space. Three sinks, two islands, and a couple of refrigerators are extras that further enhance self-sufficiency. Refrigerator drawers integrated into a bank of cabinets offer child-friendly access to juices, but even the main refrigerator is conveniently situated for access by cooks and noncooks.

Modern multitasking, though, can pair well with vintage charm. Traditional-style cabinetry detailed with corbels and beaded board conform to the home's historical spirit. A farm table ensures a place for everyone to gather, even though the goal of the design is to help people do their own thing.

TAILORED FOR TODAY

A 7-FOOT-LONG DINING TABLE
EXTENDS FROM THE WELL-EQUIPPED
ISLAND, ALLOWING FAMILY AND
FRIENDS TO TALK WITH THE COOK
WITHOUT GETTING IN THE WAY.
MOST OF THE UPPER CABINETS ARE
OUTFITTED WITH DIVIDED-LIGHT
GLASS DOORS, CORBELS, AND
BEADED BOARD FOR A FURNITURE-
INSPIRED LOOK THAT MIMICS A
HUTCH. BEHIND THE TABLE THE
DESK AREA WITH AN OPEN SHELVING
UNIT FORMS ANOTHER WORK ZONE.

Tailored for Today

Below: Corbels between the cabinetry and range hood form the illusion of an arched wall. Carved appliqués on the corbels provide an extra layer of interest.

Opposite: The range alcove makes great use of wall space by incorporating a niche on both sides for spices, condiments, and cooking oils.

PORTSMOUTH

LEFT: THE DEEP APRON-FRONT SINK AND VINTAGE-LOOK CABINETRY GIVE THE ROOM AN AGED APPEARANCE. MODERN CONVENIENCES, SUCH AS THE DISHWASHER AND A PULLOUT CABINET FOR RECYCLABLES, BLEND INTO THE NOSTALGIC SETTING.

BELOW: THE BUILT-IN HUTCH SUGGESTS A FREESTANDING FURNITURE PIECE. BUT WITH A SINK AND REFRIGERATOR DRAWERS, IT'S A MODERN BEVERAGE STATION.

Light Show

Closed off from natural light decades ago in a whole-house renovation, this kitchen regains its sparkle and its graceful Southern charm.

Left: Glass-front cabinet doors carry a light look to the ceiling.

Opposite: Windows, including transoms and sidelights on interior doorways, visually expand the kitchen. The centrally placed island that houses the sink captures views and breezes from the French doors opposite it.

LIGHT SHOW

ALTHOUGH MODERN, A SUBSTANTIAL GAS RANGE AND HOOD HAVE A CLASSIC, TIMELESS LOOK. THE STAINLESS STEEL BREAKS UP THE EXPANSE OF WHITE. OTHER APPLIANCES ARE COVERED IN PANELS, ALLOWING THE RANGE TO BE THE FOCAL POINT.

If personal ads devoted sections to people looking for their soul-mate kitchens, queries might read something like *Wanted: open and light-filled space for cooking and relaxing*. The owners of this kitchen were desperately seeking both—and managed to unearth those key attributes despite the room's small size.

The 1790 home, built to fit a narrow city lot, is a one-room-wide structure known as a Charleston single. When the primary light source—a piazza that spanned one side of the house—was closed in decades ago, the 18×13-foot kitchen seemed to grow smaller. The solution? First turn back time by restoring the piazza to its open-air glory, then link the kitchen to the piazza via French doors that let natural light penetrate the interior. A second change offers an equally significant impact: Removing a fire escape and installing a large window at the back of the house turned a drab space into a sunny sitting area that flows into the kitchen.

Interior changes also eke out light. Removing a low false ceiling gave the kitchen volume. Now glass-front cabinets climb to the ceiling to provide storage without the mass of solid doors, and transom windows above interior doorways draw in more light. A bonus in the lightening-up process: The kitchen now suggests an era of fine craftsmanship. Sure there are glimpses of modernity but this marriage between past and present is designed to last.

OPPOSITE: Square panes in upper cabinet doors offset the room's long, narrow shape and rectangular details, such as the Shaker-style cabinets.

LEFT: Fresh flowers and a large French poster flavor the kitchen with color.

BELOW: Cabinets feature cup-style pulls and latches for vintage authenticity. The hardware's nickel-plated finish complements the stainless-steel range and gives the kitchen a little extra sparkle.

Sleek
Sophistication

4

Elegantly Contoured

SWEEPING CURVES LEND A SENSE OF MOVEMENT, AND ARTFUL POLISHING NURTURES THE BEAUTY OF THIS ORGANIC-INSPIRED KITCHEN.

LEFT: ROUNDED EDGES ON THE GRANITE COUNTERTOPS ARE A SMALL DETAIL THAT FURTHERS THE CURVED THEME.

OPPOSITE: THE COFFERED CEILING AND HALF-WALL CARRY THE KITCHEN'S CIRCULAR THEME TO THE DINING AREA. DETAILING IN THE CUBIST-STYLE ARTWORK SHARES SIMILAR CONTOURS WITH THE CABINETRY AND SHELVES.

ELEGANTLY CONTOURED

THREE STEPPED CRESCENT-SHAPE SECTIONS FORM THE SHOWPIECE ISLAND. THE BANK OF CABINETS FOLLOWS THE CONTOURS. A POLE-MOUNTED SHELF CONTINUES THE THEME OF MULTILEVEL CURVES, AS DOES THE MIX OF CEILING LIGHT FIXTURES.

More than any other room, kitchens have a tendency to be a little boxy. It's a natural occurrence in a space filled with rectangular cabinets and islands. This kitchen, however, steps out of the box with a curve-slinging design.

The swoops, swerves, and circles that make this space such a standout highlight the freeflowing forms and beauty of nature. Waves of curved cabinets, countertops, and shelves impart a continual sense of movement; neutral colors let the organic shapes do the talking.

The centerpiece is a curvaceous three-tier island that incorporates exotic zebrawood in the cooktop section, stainless steel in the prep area, and fractured glass on the breakfast bar. Everything emanates from the island. A bank of cabinets along one wall forms a gentle arc, casting sweeping sight lines. Like the island, the perimeter countertops ebb and flow in height, much like hills on a horizon.

Although the appliances lack exacting curves, they're seamlessly incorporated. A curved shelf over the refrigerator and built-in ovens create a rounded appearance, as do the appliances' curved handles. Elsewhere, rounded cabinet door pulls and countertop edges transform otherwise linear elements. As is so often the case, it's the attention to detail that makes the ambitious design work—coaxing the room's few flat planes into undulation.

LEFT: THE TONE-ON-TONE ABSTRACT DESIGN OF THE CURVED FLOOR-TO-CEILING CABINET COMPLEMENTS THE VARIATIONS IN THE TRAVERTINE FLOOR.

ABOVE: GREEN-CAST FRACTURED GLASS GIVES THE BREAKFAST COUNTER A GRAPHIC APPEARANCE. A TRIPLE LAYER OF THE GLASS LENDS DIMENSION AND SUBSTANCE.

ELEGANTLY CONTOURED

BELOW: CRESCENT-SHAPE GLASS SHELVES ECHO THE CURVES OF THE UPPER CABINETS. THE ZEBRAWOOD BACKDROP LINKS TO THE ISLAND.

OPPOSITE: A STAINLESS-STEEL-CLAD CYLINDER ELEVATES THE ISLAND'S PREP AREA SO THAT IT PARTIALLY CONCEALS THE COOKTOP. WOOD TRIM AT THE BASE PREVENTS THE SLEEK PIECE FROM LOOKING TOO SPACE-AGE.

Steely Resolve

Remodeling ingenuity transforms a traditional kitchen into an industrial-strength space. Gray lacquer and shiny metal sparks the modern look.

Left: This swinging door with a round window recalls the industrial movement of the 1950s and also conjures diner-era nostalgia.

Opposite: A glossy automobile lacquer finish and elongated silvery cabinet pulls give existing cabinets a modern edge.

STEELY RESOLVE

A GRAY FINISH AND STAINLESS-STEEL TOUCHES ENHANCE THE EXISTING ISLAND. THE DOWNDRAFT COOKTOP ELIMINATES THE NEED FOR A VIEW-BLOCKING HOOD. WITH A TABLE ATTACHED TO THE ISLAND, THERE'S ROOM FOR A BUFFET.

Remodeling projects sometimes require fitting square pegs into round holes. In this kitchen the challenge was to give a toe-the-line traditional space a contemporary kick. Gutting the space wasn't an option, but ingenuity was.

The cabinets—the bane of many kitchens—were the biggest challenge. Their formal look was out of sync with the retro-modern space the owners envisioned. Since the cabinets were only two years old, it was impossible to justify tearing them out. It turns out there was no need: Sprayed with glossy automobile lacquer and outfitted with slender stainless-steel pulls, the cabinets have a sleek new look.

Creative repackaging spills over to other parts of the room too. On the island, new flush-front drawers, stainless-steel handles, and stainless-steel legs veer the existing granite countertop to the modern side. Upper cabinet doors in the pantry area give way to stainless-steel and glass doors, while the existing upper cabinet interiors, crown molding, and lower cabinets are splashed a jaunty red.

Similar bold strokes pop out here and there, warming the grays and stainless steel. A neon yellow shade stretches over an industrial-look fixture above the island. Stools at the table wear a geometric-print fabric that gives the once-traditional, now-modern kitchen another flashback to the '50s.

LEFT: SPRAYED WITH A RED CAR-BODY FINISH, THE CLASSIC BEADED-BOARD BACKING INSIDE THE CABINETS ASSUME A MOD NEW LOOK. THE VIBRANT HUE IS VISIBLE THROUGH NEW STAINLESS-STEEL DOORS WITH WIRE-EMBEDDED GLASS.

OPPOSITE: ROLLING HEIGHT-ADJUSTABLE STOOLS DESIGNED FOR DRAFTING TABLES PLAY OFF THE ROOM'S INDUSTRIALISM. THE LIVELY FABRIC ON THE SEATS AND BACKS MAKES THE OFFICE STOOLS SEEM MORE HOMEY. CABINETRY NEAR THE TABLE FUNCTIONS AS A BUTLER'S PANTRY.

OPPOSITE: THE QUILTED STAINLESS-STEEL BACKSPLASH HAS A PLAYFUL YET NOSTALGIC QUALITY. COUNTERTOP APPLIANCES AND ACCESSORIES FIT RIGHT IN WITH THE RED AND SILVERY GRAY COLOR SCHEME.

BELOW: SMOOTH STAINLESS-STEEL COUNTERTOPS PROVIDE SUBTLE TONE-ON-TONE CONTRAST TO THE QUILTED STAINLESS-STEEL BACKSPLASHES AND GRAY LACQUER-FINISH CABINETS.

Attracting Opposites

CONTEMPORARY COOLNESS AND VINTAGE WARMTH CONVERGE TO CREATE A SLICK WORKING KITCHEN THAT LOOKS LIKE IT HAS BEEN DROPPED INTO AN OLD HOME.

LEFT: NO TWO TILES ARE ALIKE IN THIS HANDPAINTED ITALIAN BACKSPLASH BEHIND THE RANGE. THE FOCAL-POINT PIECE IS THE ROOM'S ONLY COLOR PUNCH.

OPPOSITE: RUSTIC AND SLEEK SURFACES MAKE THE KITCHEN SEEM LIKE AN OLD SPACE THAT'S BEEN UPDATED. AT FLOOR LEVEL LARGE ANTIQUE TRAVERTINE TILES MEET SLEEK STAINLESS STEEL.

Attracting Opposites

MODERN CHAIRS SIDLE
UP TO AN ANTIQUE TABLE,
ECHOING THE KITCHEN'S
THEME OF CONTRASTS.
THE SALVAGED BRICK
WALL SUGGESTS VINTAGE
ARCHITECTURE, WHILE
THE STAINLESS-STEEL
ISLAND IS CLEARLY A
MODERN ADDITION.

Living in the modern world doesn't mean giving up the past. As this contemporary-meets-vintage kitchen shows, the past and present can coexist and even thrive. Here slick and modern unabashedly integrate with old and warm to create a fresh, fun, and surprising setting.

The kitchen's contemporary flavor shines through in the stainless-steel island, work area, and appliances—all set up for restaurant-style efficiency. Their sleek look is quickly tempered by the room's vintage-inspired shell. Rough and raw salvaged brick spans one wall, large antique travertine tiles cover the floor, and other walls wear a classic white Venetian stucco. But sometimes the boundaries between nostalgic and state of the art are blurred—particularly where the roll-up stainless-steel cabinet doors are inset directly into the brick wall.

Another juxtaposition plays out in the backsplashes. On one wall, the backsplash is handpainted Italian tiles; on another it's stainless steel. Classic shapes are reinterpreted in fresh ways too. Above the dining table, for example, reproduction milk bottles are fashioned into contemporary chandeliers. The eyecatching light fixtures are whimsical clues that this kitchen likes to play with the past.

Opposite: Teak countertops and stucco walls are warm counterpoints to the restaurant-style stainless steel in the primary work area.

Above: Windows in the family room bring light into the kitchen. The teak island top can serve as a buffet for easy entertaining in the combined space.

Above: Tambour doors flanking the range open to reveal storage areas with adjustable metal shelves and electrical outlets for small appliances.

Opposite: A stainless-steel rod for hanging pots and utensils spans the backsplash, integrating a touch of sleekness with the older surface.

Artful Adaptation

Modern artwork inspires the bold colors, unique shapes, and mix of surfaces that paint this kitchen as a culinary masterpiece.

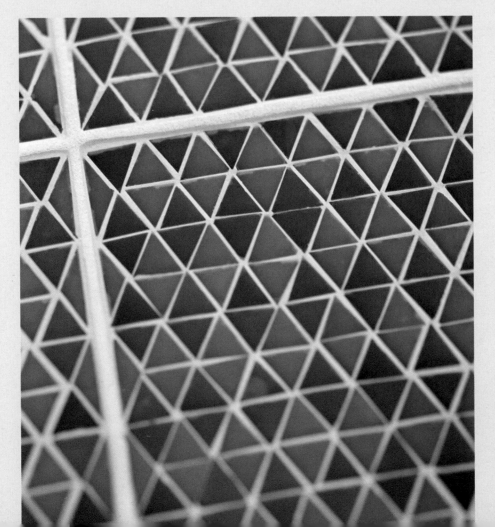

Left: Colorful handmade glass mosaic tiles make a dramatic statement above the cooktop.

Opposite: Like a work of art, the kitchen reveals nuances on close viewing. Tactile surfaces include vented metal drawer panels, textured glass on some cabinet doors, resilient bamboo flooring, and African wenge on the desk.

Artful Adaptation

THE SCULPTURAL
CURVES OF THE
BANQUETTE AND ISLAND
ARTFULLY CONTRAST
WITH THE GRIDS OF
THE COOKING AREA,
WHICH IS PUNCTUATED
BY AMETHYST-COLOR
CABINETRY. BRONZE-
FINISH TRIM LINKS THE
MIXED CABINETRY.

It's often said that a room is a blank canvas waiting to be brought to life with paint, fabric, and artwork. Kitchens, however, are less easily transformed. With limited wall space and few opportunities to use fabric, the decorating canvas may be diminished to a backsplash or sliver of wall space. This kitchen redefines conventional thinking by treating every surface—cabinetry, floors, seating—as a work of art. The result? A colorful modern masterpiece.

The room's bold shapes and vibrant colors mimic a piece of abstract art. Sweeping curves define the focal-point island, which gracefully incorporates an attached arc-shape banquette. In contrast glass tiles above the cooktop form an angular gridded backsplash. And the gold walls have nothing on the room's most striking contemporary punch: metal cabinets painted amethyst.

A combination of tactile surfaces akin to a mixed-media art piece gives the kitchen the all-important elements of surprise and depth. Exotic dark African wenge wood accentuates the arc shape of the banquette. Underfoot eco-friendly bamboo visually warms the metal cabinets and stainless-steel appliances. Upper and lower cabinets are trimmed with a bronze-finish band that acts as a sort of frame for a room that is a true work of art.

LEFT: THE EFFICIENT LAYOUT PLACES PRIMARY APPLIANCES ON THE LONG WALL PARALLEL TO THE 11-FOOT-LONG SCULPTED ISLAND.

ABOVE: STRIATED-GLASS CABINET PANELS HINT AT THE CONTENTS WITHOUT FULLY SHOWCASING THEM. THE PATTERNED GLASS TIES THE CABINETRY TO THE GLASS-BLOCK WALL IN THE ENTRYWAY NEAR THE REFRIGERATOR.

ABOVE: THE ISLAND PREP SINK IS CLOSE TO THE REFRIGERATOR FOR EASY ACCESS TO PRODUCE. NEARBY, A HARDWORKING CORNER INCORPORATES A COFFEE BAR, APPLIANCE GARAGE, AND TALL PANTRY CONVENIENTLY OUTFITTED WITH PULLOUT SHELVES.

OPPOSITE: PENDANTS ABOVE THE ISLAND AUGMENT AMBIENT LIGHT FROM RECESSED CEILING FIXTURES AND NATURAL LIGHT FROM THE WINDOWS ABOVE THE SINK.

OPPOSITE: VENTED METAL FRONTS ON THE DRAWERS IN THE COOKING AREA ARE ARTISTIC AS WELL AS FUNCTIONAL. THEY PROVIDE AIR CIRCULATION FOR ONIONS, POTATOES, AND OTHER FOODS.

BELOW: THE PAINTED CABINETS PICK UP THE AMETHYST FLECKS IN THE GRANITE COUNTERTOPS. MAPLE DRAWERS SHOW THEIR NATURAL GRAIN, PROVIDING CONTRAST TO THE SMOOTH-FINISH METAL CABINETS.

Warming Trend

Who says contemporary must be at odds with cozy? This kitchen wraps rich wood and modern detailing into a warm, inviting package.

Left: Embedding marbles into concrete, then slicing the surface to reveal the glass sections, yields this colorful countertop.

Opposite: Windows influenced by Prairie-style architecture complement the kitchen's clean lines. Horizontally installed cabinet pulls echo the window detailing, drawing the eye around the room.

WARMING TREND

Raising the ceiling 8 inches distinguishes the island and breakfast bar as command central. The ribbed-glass door to the right of the refrigerator leads to the pantry, outfitted with a counter that doubles as a desk.

Contemporary design has a reputation for being cold and stark. It's anything but in this kitchen, which incorporates a diverse mix of traditional and sleek materials.

The cherry cabinets that line the perimeter of the room give off a warm, rich glow. Although cherry is a surprising choice for a contemporary design, flat-panel cabinet doors and drawers keep the look clean. The abundant wood also offsets outwardly modern elements, such as cool stainless-steel appliances and a concrete island top embedded with colorful glass marbles. The latter touch—a playful cross between polka dots and confetti—adds the all-important element of surprise.

Yet the kitchen is for more than show. Despite being a relatively small space, it's designed for a serious cook—and serious function. The refrigerator, freezer drawers, and tall wine cooler are grouped on one wall, while the range with a restaurant-style hood anchors the opposite wall. Two dishwasher drawers plus a full-size unit make cleanup easy. Plus there's lighting for every task and every work area, thanks to an impressive 15 recessed lights that augment three pendants above the island. Set on dimmers, the lights allow the room to shift between warm and cozy or cool and bright—echoing the design itself.

LEFT: AN INKY BACKDROP OF BLACK GRANITE COUNTERTOPS AND BACKSPLASHES MAKES THE APPLIANCES SEEM SCULPTURAL. STAINLESS STEEL AND RIBBED GLASS, AS WELL AS AN ABUNDANCE OF LIGHTING, PREVENT THE COUNTERTOP AREA FROM BECOMING A BLACK HOLE.

BELOW: RIBBED-GLASS DOORS ON THE UPPER CABINETS THAT FLANK THE RANGE ARTFULLY DISTORT THE TRADITIONAL DISHES AND GLASSES STORED THERE.

Midcentury Marvel

A GALLEY-STYLE KITCHEN THAT IS SHORT ON STYLE GETS A MODERN MAKEOVER WHILE PROUDLY HONORING ITS '50S ROOTS.

LEFT: SHAPELY BARSTOOLS FIT RIGHT IN WITH THE SCULPTURAL LOOK OF MIDCENTURY MODERN STYLE.

OPPOSITE: AN ABUNDANCE OF STAINLESS STEEL DRAWS ON THE INDUSTRIALISM OF THE 1950S. FOR EFFICIENCY THE RANGE REPLACES SEPARATED COOKTOP AND OVEN UNITS.

MIDCENTURY MARVEL

THE NEWLY WIDENED DOORWAY EXPANDS THE KITCHEN AND OPENS IT TO THE HOME'S ENTRY. THE RED WALL, WHERE THE REFRIGERATOR WAS FORMERLY LOCATED, AND BRAZILIAN CHERRY FLOORING VISUALLY WARM THE INDUSTRIAL-LOOK ELEMENTS.

As far as houses go, a 1950s ranch is about as basic—and widespread—as they come. Although this house had the trademark light-challenged galley-style kitchen, it now breaks with its style-deprived design. Sure, the kitchen is still a galley-style throwback to the 1950s, but it's been remodeled into an airy midcentury gem with plenty of room to move and function.

The first order of business was to trade '50s claustrophobic for 21st-century openness. Removing one wall and narrowing another made the kitchen the eyecatching hub of the main level. White cabinetry opens the space, and the reconfigured appliance layout and new island helps the room belie its galley-style layout.

The marriage between retro and contemporary reveals itself on a number of levels. The laminated island is inspired by a 1950s Eames table, and stainless-steel countertops and appliances draw on the industrialization of the period. Other things ignore the past. The washer and dryer were relocated from the basement to the kitchen, where they are cleverly concealed in lower cabinetry—a move that pushes the envelope on conventional thinking, just as ranch-style houses did decades ago.

Midcentury marvel

Left: Glossy laminate cabinets brighten the room, as does a lack of upper cabinets. The pantry near the refrigerator makes up for lost storage space. Aluminum Eames chairs upholstered in white leather team with a 1970s table.

Below: Cabinet doors conceal the washer and dryer, moved from the basement to this handy and compact location.

Midcentury marvel

Below: Relocated to the island and mounted above the countertop, the long sink and its dramatic restaurant-style faucet stand out in the center of the room.

Opposite: The pot rack is a playful window valance. Laminated glass on the pantry doors is a durable alternative to standard glass—an important safeguard on frequently used doors.

Country-Style Comfort

5

Perfectly Imperfect

CHALLENGED WITH SLOPED CEILINGS, THIS KITCHEN STEPS UP TO THE PLATE TO CREATE A FUNCTIONAL SPACE WITH AN UNFITTED LOOK.

LEFT: AS A CONTRAST TO THE BLACK CABINETS, UNPAINTED CABINETRY SHOWS IMPERFECTIONS. THE PLATE RACK AND GLASS-FRONT DOORS KEEP DISHES IN CLEAR VIEW.

OPPOSITE: CHICKEN WIRE AND THE APRON-FRONT SINK MAKE TWO BIG COUNTRY-STYLE STATEMENTS. THE MIX OF CABINET FINISHES PROVIDES UNFITTED CHARM.

Perfectly Imperfect

In a perfect world—or at least in a perfect house—walls and floors would all be level, making remodeling projects easier. In this kitchen perfection was out of the question, given the room's sloped ceilings and unconventional location in a half-story over a garage. The dilemma? How to fill the awkward room with charm and—most daunting—function.

The 1936 Colonial could easily pull off a country look, where perfectly matched elements aren't prized. So the design approach was akin to putting together a puzzle, trying pieces here and there to create a working kitchen. The hefty range and hood claims the only tall wall. The refrigerator is pushed as close to a slope as possible, then a pantry cabinet slides in to bridge the gap between the appliance and the wall. Some cabinets are creatively custom-fit to the angles. With so much finagling required of anything that goes along the perimeter, it's no wonder the center island is loaded with function. It houses the primary sink and dishwasher and offers ample storage.

The charm phase is the easy part. Salvaged wide-plank pine lumber replaces layers of flooring. Cabinets were countrified with a distressed finish and chicken wire. A folk art tile mural on the range backsplash brings color and refinement to a kitchen that will never be perfect—and that's its beauty.

OPPOSITE: FOLK
ART TILES ARTFULLY
CONCEAL STORAGE
NICHES THAT FLANK
THE RANGE.

RIGHT: A SECONDARY
SINK BELOW THE
DORMERED WINDOW
BENEFITS FROM
NATURAL LIGHT.

Below: The desk and cabinet are simple takes on built-in office areas. Pressed-tin panels bring texture into the mix.

Opposite: Two perimeter walls incorporate an L-shape bench that supplements seating at the dining table.

Relaxed and Refined

POLISHED GRANITE AND FLUTED TRIM. KNOTTY PINE AND EXPOSED BRICK. THERE'S A PLACE FOR ALL OF THEM IN THIS WELCOMING COUNTRY FRENCH KITCHEN.

LEFT: BLUE AND PURPLE STREAKS IN THE RICHLY VEINED GRANITE EXPRESS THE COUNTRY FRENCH LOOK.

OPPOSITE: THE BRICK FIREPLACE SURROUND IS A RUGGED CONTRAST TO THE REFINED MANTEL. WALLS FLANKING THE FIREPLACE HAVE BEEN REMOVED TO OPEN THE KITCHEN TO THE FAMILY ROOM.

RELAXED AND REFINED

COLLECTIBLE BLUE-
AND-WHITE CHINA AND
PEWTER PIECES GIVE
THE ROOM A COZY
QUALITY. THE SUBWAY
TILE BACKSPLASH AND
EXPOSED HINGES ON THE
CABINETS CONTRIBUTE
VINTAGE CHARM.

Country French style offers the rare opportunity to have it both ways: elegant and homey. This sunny kitchen, with its classic yellow and blue, displays the versatility of the style that welcomes knotty pine as readily as polished granite.

The pine island, brick fireplace, and yellow pantries with doors outfitted with chicken wire are big votes for rusticity. In contrast granite countertops, formal white cabinetry, and a classically detailed mantel and range hearth move the design toward elegant. Finishing details give glimpses of the contrasts. Take the fabrics: On the built-in hutch doors, it's blue-and-white gingham; on the windows, it's elegant toile. The unmatched, casual-meets-formal approach yields an evolved-over-time look.

A less-evolved element is the floor plan, which was revamped into an efficient and modern workspace. Removing walls that flanked the fireplace opens the kitchen to the family room, creating a great room with a bit of separation. Appliances are grouped on two adjacent walls, conveniently located near each other and the dining room. The island anchors the layout, offering extra seating and workspace.

While inviting to a cook, the kitchen's comforting quality caters to noncooks too. Displays of delft pottery and pewter pieces contribute a lived-in look. And when there's a crackling fire, the kitchen is the place to be.

ABOVE: THE COOKING AREA EXUDES ELEGANCE, THANKS TO THE POLISHED GRANITE AND SHELF ABOVE THE STOVE.

OPPOSITE: PANELED DETAILING ON THE CABINETS AND THE TOILE SHADE BRING AN AIR OF FORMALITY INTO THE KITCHEN.

LEFT: BASKETS, A COUNTRY STORAGE FAVORITE, WEAVE TEXTURE INTO THE KITCHEN. THEY'RE INSET INTO PULLOUT UNITS AND LEFT EXPOSED FOR FUNCTION AND STYLE.

OPPOSITE: OLD-WORLD STYLE PREVAILS HERE. THE HEFTY TABLE GROUNDS THE LIGHT SCHEME. MATTE-FINISH LIMESTONE FLOORING IS A CASUAL CONTRAST TO THE GRANITE COUNTERTOPS.

ABOVE: BUILT-IN HUTCHES FLANK THE DOORWAY TO A MUDROOM. CHECKED FABRIC INSIDE DOORS WITH CHICKEN WIRE INSERTS ADDS A CLASSIC COUNTRY FRENCH TOUCH.

OPPOSITE: VINTAGE-LOOK WAVY-GLASS PANELS ON THE DISPLAY CABINETS NEAR THE SINK ARE ELEGANT CONTRASTS TO THE CHICKEN WIRE ON THE PANTRY DOORS.

Rugged Expression

THE RUSTIC BEAUTY OF A MOUNTAIN RETREAT COMBINES WITH EUROPEAN REFINEMENT IN A KITCHEN THAT IS AS QUAINT AS IT IS RICH IN CHARACTER.

LEFT: THE SOAPSTONE COUNTERTOP SECTIONS THAT FLANK THE COOKTOP ARE DEEP ENOUGH FOR STORING AND MEASURING INGREDIENTS.

OPPOSITE: ADDING A BANQUETTE IN THE DINING NOOK WHERE A TABLE AND CHAIRS ONCE STOOD FREES SPACE FOR A LONGER ISLAND.

RUGGED EXPRESSION

COLORFUL TREATMENTS
AND RUSTIC TOUCHES,
SUCH AS KNOTTY PINE
AND CHICKEN WIRE,
OFFER DISTINCTIVE
STORAGE. THE MANTEL
CONCEALS THE RANGE
HOOD AND BALANCES
THE FIREPLACE IN THE
ADJACENT FAMILY ROOM.

Design inspiration comes from many places—a favorite piece of art, fabric, or color. In this cottage it comes from memories rather than something material. Vacations to Colorado are the origin of this Rockies-inspired design.

Pine cabinetry and reclaimed barnwood flooring help transform the kitchen into a mountain getaway. European country elements, such as the corbel-accented mantel hood and chicken-wire inserts on some cabinets, further the rustic look. Topped with the mantel, the black soapstone backsplash above the cooktop conjures a firebox and crackling fires after a day on the slopes. More cabin-inspired coziness comes from the 9-foot-long island and armoire-style pantry, both of which wear a distressed red finish.

Like a remote cabin that needs to be well-stocked in case of storms, the design packs plenty of function into a small area. Four pullouts near the cooktop incorporate utensil holders, tall shelves for oils and wines, and shelves for spices. The pantry offers an array of storage, as does the island and a beverage center. The slim 27-inch-wide refrigerator was chosen to encourage cooking with fresh ingredients from a nearby market—a perk that's possible because this kitchen is a mountain getaway only in spirit.

OPPOSITE: THE
KITCHEN SPILLS INTO
THE FAMILY ROOM,
WHERE A BUILT-IN
BEVERAGE CENTER
REPLACES CLOSETS.
THE CENTER OFFERS
PLENTIFUL STORAGE
AND DISPLAY SPACE.

RIGHT: DISHWASHER
DRAWERS AND
CABINETS MAKE
THE ISLAND A
HARDWORKING
ADDITION. THE
FIRECLAY SINK
RESISTS ABRASION.

LEFT: STORAGE SPACE TOPS THE LIST OF POSITIVES IN THIS KITCHEN DESIGN. AN ARRAY OF SHELVES AND DRAWERS MAKES THE PANTRY STORAGE-CENTRAL.

OPPOSITE: THE STAGGERED CABINET HEIGHTS PROVIDE VISUAL INTEREST AND DISTINGUISHES THE RED PANTRY AS THE FOCAL POINT.

Formal Abandon

Rough textures and rich colors make intriguing companions in this traditional kitchen that embraces a surprising amount of rusticity.

Left: Chicken wire casts a rustic pattern over a creamware urn in a cabinet used as a display case.

Opposite: zinc, copper, and wrought iron form a machine-shed mix of metals on and above the farm table.

FORMAL ABANDON

Country and traditional styles are filled with contrasts—one is primitive, the other prim. In this kitchen, the two styles gracefully unite to create a character-rich space with a comforting, stay-awhile quality.

The unique look begins with the rough-hewn island centerpiece. It's actually a zinc-top antique farm table retrofitted with a sink to launch the room's informal style. The perimeter of the room is all about classic elegance. A taupe glaze tints creamy cabinetry, Chinese toile wallpaper dresses the walls, and brown granite countertops are a polished contrast to the zinc. In the dining area an upholstered bench and chairs give the room a manicured quality.

Credit for the stylistic blending goes, in part, to the intriguing layers set against a sophisticated cream-and-coffee color scheme. This is a kitchen where decorating is more than an afterthought—and it shows in the ambience that makes the kitchen as cozy as the other rooms in the home. Throw pillows on the bench and wicker baskets on the walls layer the room with warmth. Drapery panels in the dining area strike a traditional note, while a basket holding vintage rolling pins takes things back to the country.

ABOVE: REWIRED AND HUNG NEAR THE
MIRROR, AGED SCONCES COMPLEMENT THE
CURVES IN THE WALLPAPER MOTIFS.

Formal Abandon

BELOW: ANTIQUE WICKER BASKETS AND GALVANIZED BUCKETS COMPLEMENT THE WEATHERED PATINA OF THE TABLE ISLAND.

OPPOSITE: MATCHING THE ISLAND TOP, THE ZINC SINK DISPLAYS THE PRIMITIVE SIDE OF THIS KITCHEN'S DESIGN.

Finely Grained

Elegant cherry cabinetry steeps a country kitchen in tradition yet harmonizes with knotty pine and farm-fresh tile accents.

Left: Detailing on the feet and drawers gives the island the look of a fine cabinet. The narrow arched door fronts a spice rack.

Opposite: An arched doorway marks the transition from the knotty pine used throughout the home to the kitchen's curly cherry. The quartersawn oak floor is a rich complement.

FINELY GRAINED

THE TILE MURAL NEAR THE OVENS BRINGS VISUAL RELIEF TO THE SEA OF CABINETRY. THE MURAL IS BASED ON A PAINTING. SHELVES AT BOTH ENDS OF THE SPACIOUS ISLAND CAN ACCOMMODATE OVERFLOW ITEMS.

Country kitchens often bring to mind distressed cabinetry, primitive farm tables, and other rough-hewn surfaces. This kitchen turns the tables with an impressive display of rich cherry. Although the abundance of wood is steeped in tradition, this kitchen has its heart in the country. Hints of farmlife come into focus upon closer look.

Tile backsplashes and china displayed against the elegant wood play off the home's rural setting. Barnyard animals and rural scenes grace the handpainted tile murals and china pieces, relaxing the room's formality. Wide windows behind the sink take in relaxing country views, enhancing the kitchen's connection to its setting.

While the murals are showpieces, the woodwork itself also has an artful quality. Carpenters worked tediously to match the distinctive roping patterns of the curly cherry on cabinets and millwork for a consistent and seamless look. Cabinetry and the room-anchoring island are detailed to resemble elegant freestanding furniture pieces. Fine artistry is also evident in the arches and beefy moldings that represent the home's Colonial Revival style.

OPPOSITE: VERMONT SLATE COUNTERTOPS ARE A HOMEGROWN ELEMENT. VINTAGE-STYLE FAUCETS ADD AUTHENTICITY.

ABOVE: WOOD PANELS HIDE THE ICEMAKER AND DISHWASHER IN THE PREP AREA FACING THE FAMILY ROOM.

LEFT: THE SINK BACKSPLASH INCORPORATES COUNTRY IMAGERY. ARCH-TOP TOWEL NOOKS BELOW THE SINK ARE DOORLESS TO IMPROVE AIR CIRCULATION FOR QUICK DRYING.

BELOW: SIMPLY SHAPED NICKEL HARDWARE COMPLEMENTS THE RAISED PANELS ON THE CABINET DOORS.

Sunshine State

Light, bright, and outfitted with perky yellow cabinets, this kitchen is the go-to place to soothe the soul as well as nourish the body.

Left: Tiles inset on each side of the sink backsplash provide a fun splash of color and pattern.

Opposite: An expansive farm table ensures that there is plenty of room for guests. The antique icebox and chandelier contrast with the formal frame on the painting.

Sunshine State

The mark of good design is its ability to evoke emotion. With buttery yellow walls and abundant natural light, this kitchen succeeds as a feel-good place. Sunny, happy, and inviting are fitting descriptions of the Colonial-inspired design.

The renovation started off a little too ambitious. After the painted maple cabinetry was installed, the room was a bit too sunny. To tone down the brightness, blue granite countertops were brought in for moderation, then reds and greens were used as accent colors for European flavor.

From a decorating standpoint the spacious layout offers room to play. The range backsplash features a pastoral scene of grazing cattle and rolling fields. A collection of antiques fills the room with a comforting and homey quality rarely found in today's kitchens.

Functionality is where the design really excels. The butler's pantry is outfitted with a big stainless-steel sink that keeps soaking pots out of view from guests. The island incorporates an undercounter refrigerator for storing produce where it's prepared. And one of the island's chunky turned legs is recessed with an electric outlet.

With so much function and style seamlessly blended into one space, the sunny kitchen naturally elicits smiles.

LEFT: RARE TANZANIAN BLUE GRANITE COUNTERTOPS CUT THE BRIGHTNESS OF THE YELLOW CABINETS. MATCHING LIGHT FIXTURES ABOVE THE ISLAND HAVE BEEN RETROFITTED FOR ELECTRICITY.

ABOVE: THE MANTEL ABOVE THE COOKTOP IS MORE THAN A DISPLAY SPACE. ITS RECESSED LIGHTS ILLUMINATE THE COOKING AREA.

Global Influence 6

Glimpses of Provence

Earthy textures and a welcoming connection to the outdoors imbue this American kitchen with charming South-of-France flavor.

Left: The aged brass-finish fixtures will develop a rich patina over time.

Opposite: The breakfast room is a solarium in the spirit of Provençal orangeries—rooms that often store citrus trees during the winter.

GLIMPSES OF PROVENCE

There's a certain romance to a kitchen choreographed with the South of France in mind. It conjures beautiful scenery; flavorful cuisine enriched with homegrown herbs, olives, figs, or lemons; and a casual lifestyle that embraces the indoor-outdoor connection.

The lucky owners of this kitchen would agree. The space is like a snapshot of old-school Provence imported into a modern American home. The focus is on celebrating nature. Doors and windows are meant to be flung open to bring the fresh air inside, and the glass-walled breakfast area is the next best thing to dining alfresco. Within the four walls, earthy textures stand in for nature. Stoneware pottery pieces are displayed on a shelving unit and the mantel above the range. French artisans crafted the island and stools from raw sycamore, a self-healing wood that requires no protective coating.

For all its Mediterranean glory, the kitchen also features homegrown nuances. The deep farmhouse sink and ceiling beams are actually hallmarks of American country kitchens. Also homebred is the kitchen's layout, which ensures plenty of space for cooking and gathering. After all American kitchens—even when they emulate the French countryside—are designed for efficiency.

ESCHEWING UPPER CABINETS FOR SHELVES—OR SIMPLY LEAVING WALLS BARE—IS A FARMHOUSE TRADITION. HANDMADE STONEWARE DISPLAYED ON THE SHELVES COORDINATES WITH THE COLORFUL CHECKERBOARD-TILE BACKSPLASH, AND BASKETS ADD A LAYER OF TEXTURE. THE BACKSPLASH TILES WERE MADE IN FRANCE.

LEFT: WITH THICK
LEGS AT THE ENDS,
THE ISLAND IS
REMINISCENT OF
THE STURDY CENTER
TABLES COMMON
IN PROVENÇAL
KITCHENS. THE
ISLAND'S CABINETS
ARE VISIBLE ONLY
TO THE COOK,
ENSURING THAT THE
PIECE LOOKS LIKE A
TABLE FROM MOST
VANTAGE POINTS.

OPPOSITE: GOLDEN-
TONE LIMESTONE
COUNTERTOPS ARE
A BRIDGE BETWEEN
THE BRIGHT TILES
AND LIGHT CABINETS.

Humble Beginning

Raw beauty and a collected-over-time look win out over polished refinement in a kitchen renovated to capture Spanish simplicity.

Left: Faux drawer fronts and carved legs give this island a furniture look. Baskets keep storage niches looking tidy.

Opposite: The Mexican tiles on the island echo the windows' grid design. For historical authenticity, small recessed windows were used instead of one large one.

Humble Beginning

INDIVIDUAL CABINET
PIECES APPEAR TO
HAVE BEEN ADDED
OVER THE YEARS.
THE BONNET-TOPPED
ARMOIRE CONCEALS
THE REFRIGERATOR.
DISHWASHERS ARE
INTEGRATED INTO
CABINETS ON BOTH SIDES
OF THE SINK.

Just as there are two sides to every story, there are several sides to each architectural and design style. Take, for example, Spanish design. It can be lushly layered with Mediterranean-inspired romance, or it can be rustic, even a bit primitive. It's the latter—the simpler side of Spanish style—that this kitchen brilliantly captures.

The somewhat utilitarian and function-first look is part of the room's charm. The floor plan takes its cue from old Spanish Revival kitchens that included several workstations for servants. The range, which claims its own cabinet-free wall, is a hardworking space intended for cooking. Modern luxuries are similarly isolated—they're hidden in cabinetry to help the kitchen retain its old-world flair.

The new architecture suggests age, as well as a keen eye for proportions. Walls that appear to be thick plaster are actually ordinary drywall that was skim-troweled. Cabinets that look like armoires and the center island have Spanish-style heft that keeps the room's size in check; the mismatched pieces also look as though they've been collected over time. Arched doorways and cedar beams on the ceiling lend more Spanish authenticity, as do materials such as Mexican tiles on the island and saltillo flooring.

As an alternative to rich reds and oranges, a palette of indigo blue, cream, and terra-cotta keeps things on the cool side, underscoring a look that some may consider raw and others may call simply elegant.

ABOVE: HONED RED TRAVERTINE COUNTERTOPS PICK UP THE BROWNS AND GOLDS OF THE UNMATCHED CUPBOARDS. PLACED DIRECTLY ON THE PENINSULA, THIS DARK-STAINED CUPBOARD ALLOWS EASY ACCESS TO PLATES.

RIGHT: ALL DOORWAYS, INCLUDING THE GLASS DOORS THAT LEAD TO A LOGGIA, ARE ARCHED FOR A UNIFIED LOOK THAT VISUALLY SOFTENS THE LARGE ROOM. AN IRON CHANDELIER AND CHAIRS SHOW THE MOORISH INFLUENCE ON SPANISH COLONIAL DESIGN. ANTIQUE CORBELS ADD DETAIL TO THE CEILING BEAMS.

Humble Beginning

Arches outfitted with recessed lights for dramatic shadowing distinguish the kitchen from the great room. Rustic cedar ceiling beams help tame the room's volume. Extra-thick skim-troweled walls suggest plaster, which is common in Spanish homes. Placed on an angle, the saltillo floor tiles provide visual relief from horizontal elements.

French Accent

Inspired by a Parisian townhouse, this kitchen brings a sense of romance and chic sophistication into everyday dining and cooking.

Left: A simple and elegant diamond motif details the kitchen cabinetry.

Opposite: The mahogany-top breakfast bar that attaches to the island is a space-saver. The bar's chunky legs visually balance the island's heft.

FRENCH ACCENT

Many rooms have a state-of-mind quality to them. With the right touches they can be anything their owners want. In this kitchen, Paris is calling. Chic, understated, and elegant, the design evokes a Parisian townhome—a *hôtel particulier*— with modern elements that are Americanized versions of classic French design.

The kitchen displays the French passion for architecture, especially stone treatment, to bring visual interest into what otherwise could be merely an ordinary American space. Scagliola—a blend of stone powders and chips shaped by hand into a decorative surface—forms the striking range hood that implies the kitchen is steeped in history and tradition. Limestone floors and marble countertops are worthy stone complements.

Understatement of color and a reliance on interesting texture are part of the appeal of French design, which plays out here beautifully. Pewter—chosen to complement the stone—powers a color scheme that includes gray-blue cabinets and shades of brown, cream, and white. Pewter in metallic form—which appears in faucets and decorative accents—acts as a bridge between old-fashioned patinas and modern chrome finishes. It's a subtle hint at the overall style, which underscores the ongoing American love affair with French design.

FRENCH ACCENT

LEFT: THE KITCHEN DRAWS ON THE PLENTIFUL NATURAL LIGHT OF THE FAMILY ROOM, WHICH FEATURES WINDOWS MADE IN PARIS. THE RAISED-DIAMOND PATTERN ON THE ISLAND CABINETRY WAS INSPIRED BY A LINEN FABRIC THAT WAS USED IN THE FAMILY ROOM.

BELOW: WITH A BRIDGE DESIGN AND GOOSENECK SPOUT, THE FAUCET HAS AN OLD FRENCH LOOK TO IT. MARBLE COUNTERTOPS WITH GRAY, GREEN, AND MERLOT VEINING PLAY OFF THE ROOM'S JUXTAPOSITION OF LIGHT AGAINST DARK.

LEFT: THE SCAGLIOLA STONE RANGE HOOD GIVES THE KITCHEN A SENSE OF AGE AND PERMANENCE. THE FIREPLACE IN THE ADJACENT FAMILY ROOM IS MADE FROM THE SAME STONE FOR CONTINUITY.

OPPOSITE: A DOOR IN WHAT APPEARS TO BE A WALL OF CABINETS OPENS TO A WALK-IN PANTRY. A MIRRORED WALL WITH PEWTER PLATES BRIGHTENS THE EXPANSE OF DARK CABINETS.

Something Borrowed

EMULATING THE MINIMALIST STYLE AND MAXIMIZED FUNCTION OF EUROPEAN DESIGN, THIS SMALL KITCHEN PUTS EVERY INCH OF SQUARE FOOTAGE TO WORK.

LEFT: A TRAY WITH SLOTS SHAPED FOR SPECIFIC UTENSILS KEEPS A COOKTOP DRAWER ORGANIZED.

OPPOSITE: FOR A STREAMLINED LOOK, THE BLACK COOKTOP RECEDES INTO THE GRANITE. THE CLEAR ITALIAN RANGE HOOD ALSO FADES INTO THE BACKGROUND.

SOMETHING BORROWED

NOT LARGE BY TODAY'S
STANDARDS, THIS
KITCHEN PROMOTES
EFFICIENCY WITH
A CENTER ISLAND
AND WOOD-PANELED
STORAGE WALL. RIFT-CUT
NATURAL CHERRY WARMS
THE LACQUER CABINETS
AND TONES DOWN THE
OVERALL SLEEKNESS.

Although it's sometimes true that everything one needs is in one's own backyard, casting a wider net often inspires ideas as yet unimagined. The designer of this compact kitchen looked abroad for inspiration. Borrowing a European penchant for packing lots of style, function, and even fun into crowded spaces, the kitchen is sleek and storage-savvy beyond its square footage.

The most noticeable "borrowed" touch is the green cabinetry. Europeans have embraced a colorful array of cabinetry for years, but Americans are slower to jump into something that takes effort to change. Knowing that steering clear of trendy is the key to longevity, these owners opted for green, a color widely regarded as one of the new neutrals.

Lively color isn't the room's only wake-up call. The cabinetry—in green lacquer as well as a rift-cut natural cherry—is from an Italian manufacturer known for clever components and smart looks. In addition to utensil trays and pullout pantries, there are extra-deep and wide drawers for heavy pots and pans. Behind the sink a trough serves as a draining board and storage place for cutting boards and knives. And the island includes a pullout baking center with a retractable mixer stand. Of course the real beauty is that such savvy storage and sleek style work for kitchens of all sizes—big, small, or somewhere in between.

OPPOSITE: SUNLIGHT STREAMS THROUGH TALL WINDOWS LEFT UNDRESSED ABOVE THE MAIN SINK. THE GREEN-AND-BURGUNDY GRANITE COUNTERTOPS INSPIRED THE LACQUER-FINISH CABINETS.

BELOW: A DOOR "HIDDEN" IN THE PRIMARY STORAGE WALL OPENS TO A PANTRY. THE SECRET ROOM IS A PLAYFUL TOUCH THAT ALLOWS THE INTERIOR CABINETRY WALLS TO BE FLUSH FOR A STREAMLINED LOOK.

ABOVE: TWO REFRIGERATORS FLANKED BY
PULLOUT PANTRIES BLEND INTO THE STORAGE
WALL. HANDLES AND PULLS ARE THE ONLY
CLUES AS TO WHAT'S WHERE.

OPPOSITE: IN TRUE EUROPEAN STYLE,
METAL LEGS ELEVATE THE CABINETRY AND
APPLIANCES FOR A FURNITURE LOOK AND A
LIGHT VISUAL APPEARANCE.

LEFT: THE TROUGH IN THE ISLAND GETS PLENTY OF USE. IT'S A DRAINAGE AND DRYING SPACE FOR JUST-WASHED DISHES AND A BUILT-IN STORAGE AREA FOR CUTTING BOARDS AND KNIVES.

ABOVE: DEEP AND WIDE DRAWERS BELOW THE COOKTOP KEEP PANS HANDY. THE DRAWERS ARE DESIGNED TO OPEN AND CLOSE EASILY, EVEN WHEN LADEN WITH HEAVY ITEMS.

Something Borrowed

Below: A shelving unit that resembles a flat-panel television makes an intriguing focal point above the buffet. The countertop also serves as a desktop and coffee bar.

Opposite: This inventive shelving unit is inspired by overhead compartments on airplanes. Lights illuminate the interior when the door is raised.

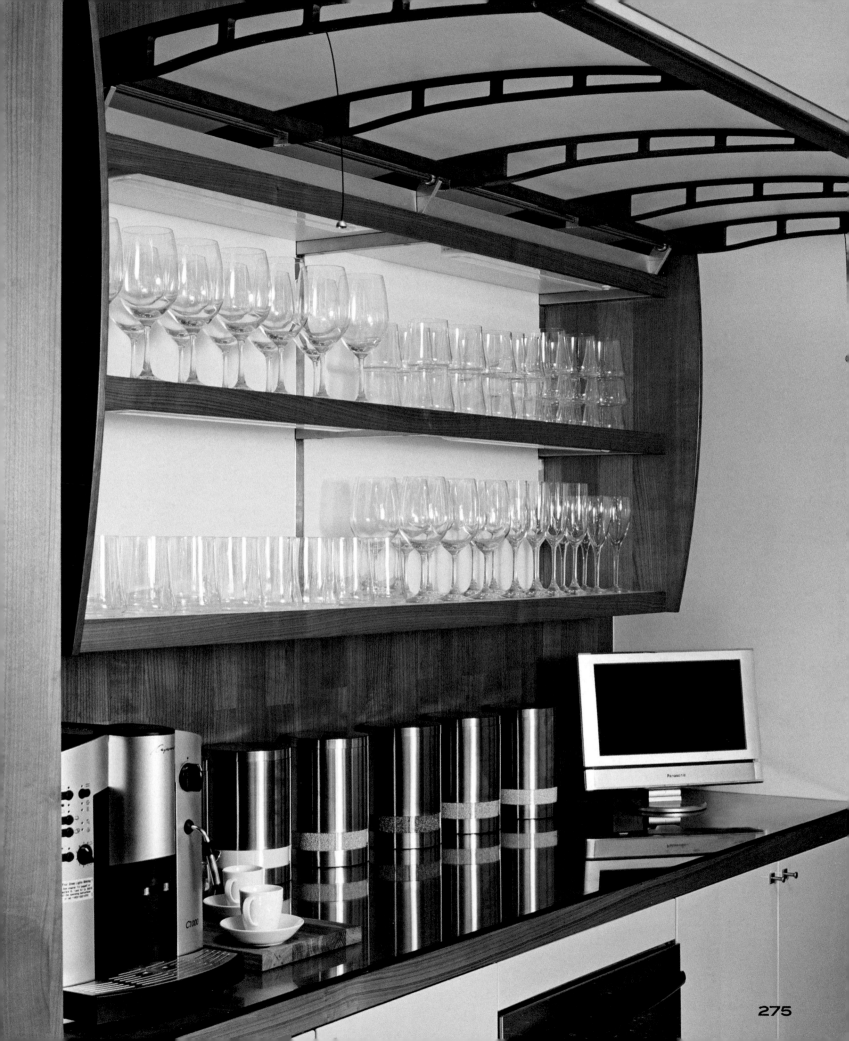

True to Tradition

Separated from other rooms, this kitchen takes a classic floor plan on a worldly journey to Portugal, Spain, and other destinations.

Left: European ceramics echo the colors and motifs of the handmade wall tiles.

Opposite: Century-old wooden doors frame a striking mosaic tile art piece when the kitchen is exposed to other rooms.

True to Tradition

Classic English-inspired cabinets are casual complements to the room's lively details, such as the Italianate insets in the island and transoms, foliate-motif backsplashes, and Mediterranean vases and pottery.

In an era when kitchens are the favorite place to congregate, it's rare to find one that's separate and not the home's focal point. The traditional, a-place-removed approach is part of the charm of this intriguing space. Fling open carved wooden doors that isolate the kitchen from other rooms and you're in another world.

Touches of Italy, England, and Portugal visually transport the kitchen and dining area to an old European villa. The worldly amalgam continues: The century-old carved doors are from India, though they have a distinctly Spanish look. Even the floor plan has a cultural reference: Everyday dining happens in a room just off the kitchen in keeping with a Mexican tradition of gathering for meals in a place other than the cooking space.

As would be expected from a design that gleans the best of different cultures, the detailing is exquisite. Foliate grillwork in the island and transoms has a Tuscan look. Pilasters and crown molding on the celestial blue cabinets are edged with creamy white paint for an aged look. Hand-painted Portuguese tiles and Mediterranean ceramics enliven the walls. Despite being part of a room designed as private quarters, a showpiece tile mural is placed so that the doors frame a beautiful view if guests desire a peek inside.

Opposite: The private dining area boldly carries the kitchen's blue-and-yellow scheme. Cabinetry further unifies the two rooms.

Left: The design brings elegant detailing to the room's higher reaches. Italianate grillwork stands in for glass in the transoms.

Below: The arched buffet area with a colorful floral mosaic is the kitchen's dramatic welcoming point.

Side of Serenity

Sculptural shapes with an Asian influence soften the angles of a 1940s Arts and Crafts kitchen, evoking calm in a chaotic world.

Left: Layers of coffee-color glazes create a warm backdrop for shapely sconces that emit a candlelike glow.

Opposite: Resilient cork flooring and pale wood cabinets launch the kitchen's organic look.

SIDE OF SERENITY

REMOVING INTERIOR
WALLS OPENS THE
KITCHEN TO THE FAMILY
ROOM. SCULPTURAL
FURNISHINGS AND
ACCESSORIES CONTRAST
WITH THE STRAIGHT
ANGLES. THE RAISED
CABINET AT THE END OF
THE ISLAND HOLDS A TV
AND ELECTRONICS.

There's a lot to be said for a style that brings a sense of calm and serenity into a busy hub like a kitchen. Such is the case with Asian design. In this kitchen Japanese-influenced minimalism and natural hues cast a Zenlike influence over a 1940s Arts and Crafts space.

The fusion of Asian and Arts and Crafts finds common ground in simplicity and an appreciation for artful forms. Geometric patterns combine curvaceous and organic with angular and strong. A gracefully curved center island and sink area take their cue from the home's original curved windows. Square and checkerboard detailing on the cabinetry and the butcher-block island countertop are updated interpretations of Arts and Crafts detailing.

By eschewing bold colors and lacquered finishes common to some Asian styles for more subdued Japanese influences, the kitchen has a quiet, comforting quality. Walls with layers of coffee-color glazes wrap the room in warmth. Pale maple cabinetry—instead of a dark wood tone common to Arts and Crafts style—capitalizes on natural light. Decorative items are sculptural, though kept to a minimum. Even the furnishings, including a cushy upholstered chair, manage to bring style and comfort into the kitchen—a lofty goal for such a hardworking room.

OPPOSITE: INSTEAD OF A HARSH L-SHAPE CORNER, MAPLE BASE CABINETS AND STAINLESS-STEEL COUNTERTOPS FORM A GENTLE CURVE. SINKS—ONE RECTANGULAR, ONE ROUND—SHOWCASE THE ROOM'S DELIGHTFUL MIX OF CURVES AND ANGLES.

ABOVE: THE PANTRY AREA ARTFULLY INTEGRATES PLENTIFUL STORAGE AND DISPLAY SPACE. THE REFRIGERATOR PANEL TO THE LEFT FEATURES HAND-CHISELED WOOD DIVIDED INTO SQUARES. THE DETAILING REPEATS ON THE CABINET BELOW THE SINKS.

OPPOSITE: CABINETRY CONCEALS TWO DISHWASHERS; ONE IS SET HIGHER FOR EASE IN LOADING AND UNLOADING DISHES. THE SHELVING UNIT—A MODERN TAKE ON A PLATE RACK—PLAYS OFF THE GRID DESIGN OF THE CABINETS AND WINDOWS.

BELOW: HANDSOME ADD-ONS ENHANCE A CORNER OF THE ISLAND. A HAND-CHISELED WOODEN BOWL, USUALLY FILLED WITH SNACKS, DROPS INTO THE BUTCHER-BLOCK COUNTERTOP. BELOW THE COUNTER A "FLOATING" DRAWER KEEPS KNIVES HANDY.

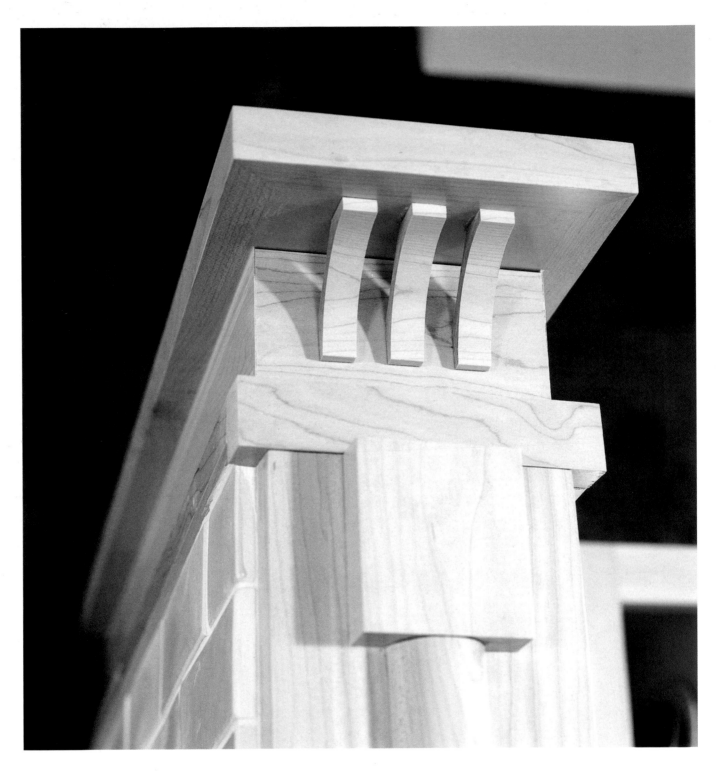

ABOVE: FINE DETAILING SETS THIS KITCHEN APART. CUSTOM MOLDING TOPS THE PARTIAL WALLS THAT DEFINE THE COOKING AREA AND HIGHLIGHTS THE REPEATING ARCHITECTURAL ELEMENTS OF SQUARES AND CIRCLES.

OPPOSITE: A COPPER-COLOR BOWL-STYLE SINK IS THE FOCAL POINT OF THE BUTLER'S PANTRY, WHICH ADJOINS THE KITCHEN. TO MAXIMIZE STORAGE SPACE IN THE CABINETS, THE ICEMAKER AND WINE CHILLER ARE INTEGRATED INTO THE WALL.

Stone Aged

THIS WELL-FORTIFIED KITCHEN USES EUROPEAN CASTLES AS ITS DESIGN MUSE, BUT ITS MEDIEVAL SPIRIT ADAPTS WELL TO MODERN LIFE.

LEFT: THE MODERN LIGHT FIXTURE RESEMBLING A CLUSTER OF CANDLES CASTS A WARM GLOW OVER THE TABLE.

OPPOSITE: ROUGH LIMESTONE WALLS AND EXPOSED CEILING TIMBERS DISPLAY FORTRESSLIKE PRESENCE. METAL CABINETS SET ON TALL LEGS ARE A VISUALLY LIGHT COUNTERPOINT.

STONE AGED

THE VIEW FROM THE SINK
IS THE BEST IN THE ROOM.
THE FREESTANDING
CABINET IS SET ON TALL
LEGS TO ALLOW NATURAL
LIGHT TO FLOW BELOW IT,
WHILE THE STAINLESS-
STEEL COUNTERTOP
REFLECTS LIGHT ABOVE.
CENTER WINDOWS OPEN
TO LET IN FRESH AIR.

Giving a new kitchen an old-world European look usually involves digging back decades—a century at best—and covering walls with Venetian plaster or a lime wash for instant age. This kitchen is more literal in its interpretation of Old World and less predictable in its surface treatments. The inspiration? Ancient castles.

Medieval spirit plays out in stone walls, a high ceiling, and arched windows. Rough limestone walls give the kitchen strength of character and a sense of being well-protected. On the focal-point wall, the stonework forms a sweeping arch that follows the shape of the windows. The windows start at the floor and rise almost to the ceiling, welcoming light in contrast to a dimly lit castle. Other contrasts ensure the kitchen isn't thematic. Sleek metal cabinetry, granite and stainless-steel countertops, and aluminum backsplashes maintain a firm footing in modern times.

Then there are elements that manage to bridge both worlds. Above the table what looks like a mass of candles that might have helped illuminate a castle is actually a contemporary light fixture that glows with the flip of a switch. And the long rustic table that takes the place of an island could go either way: One could envision lords and ladies feasting at it as easily as members of a busy family enjoying catching up with one another there at the end of the day.

OPPOSITE: THE ECLECTIC MIX OF MATERIALS LIES WITHIN PLANES FOR AN UNFUSSY LOOK. THE GRANITE COUNTERTOP AND ALUMINUM BACKSPLASH, FOR EXAMPLE, STOP AT THE CORNER. ONLY THE ROOM-DEFINING LIMESTONE WRAPS AROUND CORNERS.

ABOVE: REFLECTIVE SURFACES, INCLUDING THE STAINLESS-STEEL RANGE AND HOOD, ALUMINUM BACKSPLASH, AND ELONGATED CABINET PULLS, CREATE A BRIGHT—NOT DARK AND DUNGEONY—KITCHEN.

OPPOSITE: WIDE DRAWERS WITH HOLES FOR PEGS ARE FLEXIBLE DISHWARE ORGANIZERS. THE PEGS CAN BE MOVED TO ACCOMMODATE VARIOUS SIZES OF DISHES.

LEFT: SINK FIXTURES ARE SLEEK AND SIMPLY STYLED IN A CLEAN-LINED CONTRAST TO THE KITCHEN'S RUGGED ELEMENTS.

BELOW: FROSTED GLASS OBSCURES THE CONTENTS OF UPPER CABINETS WITHOUT THE MASS OF SOLID DOORS.

ABOVE: THE BAR AREA OFFERS CONVENIENCE WHEN ENTERTAINING. IN THE WALL, A SMALL PASS-THROUGH TO THE DINING ROOM MAKES IT EASY TO GRAB WINE BOTTLES CHILLING IN THE SINK. THE MICROWAVE OVEN IS HANDY FOR WARMING APPETIZERS.

OPPOSITE: FRENCH DOORS LINK THE KITCHEN TO A STONE TERRACE AND OUTDOOR EATING AREA. THE TABLE, WHICH TAKES THE PLACE OF AN ISLAND, IS AN INVITING CENTERPIECE. THE TORREY PINE TABLETOP IS A RUGGED CONTRAST TO THE MODERN BENCHES.

INDEX

dare to dream
be inspired and make your dream a reality

GREAT **BATHS** COLLECTION

GREAT **TRADITIONAL STYLE**

GREAT **COUNTRY FRENCH** STYLE

GREAT **WINDOWS & WALLS** COLLECTION

GREAT **COLOR & PATTERN** COLLECTION

{ Style and Inspiration combine to bring you the best design ideas.
Look for these inspiring titles where home improvement books are sold. }